中国廊桥精粹

THE QUINTESSENCE OF COVERED BRIDGES IN CHINA

《中国廊桥精粹》编写组

人民交通出版社

北 京

《中国廊桥精粹》编写组

主　　任：郑皆连

副 主 任：张劲泉　刘　杰

编 审 委：蒋响元　杨　林　漆志平　金宁帆

主　　编：吴卫平

英文翻译：东　鸿　蒋音成　李焕阳　屈天舒

The Quintessence of Covered Bridges in China Compilation Committee

Chair: Zheng Jielian

Vice-chair: Zhang Jingquan   Liu Jie

Editorial Board: Jiang Xiangyuan   Yang Lin   Qi Zhiping   Jin Ningfan

Editor-in-chief: Wu Weiping

Translators: Abraham Moses Zamcheck   Jiang Yincheng   Li Huanyang   Qu Tianshu

前 言

习近平总书记指出，考古遗迹和历史文物是历史的见证，必须保护好、利用好。中国廊桥建设历史悠久、璀璨夺目，是交通运输发展历史的见证。

中国廊桥建造史绵延两千多年。中国廊桥可追溯至西汉时期，例如，成都市金沙遗址和盐市口各出土一座建于西汉时期的木构廊桥；记述廊桥最早的文字可追溯至东汉永平六年，陕西省勉县凿刻的《开通褒斜道摩崖刻石》刻着的"桥阁六百三十二间，大桥五，为道二百五十八里"文字。此后，唐朝、五代十国、宋朝等朝代都有大量关于廊桥的文学作品，这些作品完全可以佐证中国廊桥的历史演进脉络。到了明、清两朝，中国廊桥进入黄金时期，有大量的廊桥遗存至今。本书主要收录了始建于三国至清代期间的有代表性的廊桥。

中国廊桥在漫长的历史里演化出独特的廊桥文化，这种文化里起支撑作用的是古代交通人逢山开路、遇水架桥的精神、工匠精神、社区文化等人文精神。中国廊桥具有鲜明的独创性，其建筑工艺奇妙、文化信息丰富，是中国工匠精神造就的奇迹。例如，贯木叠插别压式木拱廊桥代表了中国古代桥梁技艺的最高成就，有"无桥之桥"之誉，是中国工匠智慧的结晶和中国工匠精神的体现。此外，廊桥由于其独特的社区功能产生了一定范围内的社区文化。廊桥常常是人们遮风避雨、休息交谈的社交场所，又逐渐成为互通有无的贸易市场，后来甚至成为家族酒席、婚丧嫁娶等活动的举办场地。因此，便自然产生了基于廊桥的社区文化。中国廊桥以其深邃的文史底蕴、精美巧妙的姿容、高超的桥梁技艺将廊桥文化推向高峰。

鉴往以知来，前人的创造为后辈提供了潜移默化的文化滋养。中国廊桥是人们做出的人类与自然、生活与生产、物质与精神、资源与环境等多边性关系的解决方案，是中国古代交通人逢山开路、遇水架桥的宝贵物质遗产，更是我们在加快建设交通强国的进程中应当继承的宝贵精神财富。

编者
2024 年 9 月

PREFACE

Xi Jinping, General Secretary of the Communist Party of China (CPC) Central Committee, has pointed out that archaeological sites and historical relics are witnesses to history and must be well protected and utilized. China's covered bridges boast a long and splendid history, serving as witnesses to the development of transportation.

The history of building covered bridges in China spans over two thousand years. The origin of China's covered bridges can be traced back to the Western Han Dynasty, exemplified by the unearthed wooden covered bridges in the Jinsha Site and Yanshikou in Chengdu, both of which date back to this period. The earliest written record of covered bridges can be traced back to the sixth year of Yongping in the Eastern Han Dynasty. Since then, the Tang Dynasty, the Five Dynasties and Ten Kingdoms period, the Song Dynasty, and other dynasties have produced a large number of literary works related to covered bridges, which fully document the historical evolution of China's covered bridges. During the Ming and Qing dynasties, China's covered bridges entered a golden age, with a significant number of them preserved to this day. The book mainly includes representative covered bridges that were built from the Three Kingdoms period to the Qing Dynasty.

Over its long history, China's covered bridges have evolved into a unique covered bridge culture, which is underpinned by humanistic spirits such as the spirit of ancient transport professionals to build roads over mountains and bridges over rivers, craftsmanship, and community culture. China's covered bridges exhibit remarkable ingenuity, with exquisite architectural craftsmanship and a wealth of cultural significance, making them wonders crafted by China's craftsmanship spirit.

For instance, the timber-arch covered bridges with overlapping and interlocking timber structures represent the highest achievement of ancient Chinese bridge-building techniques, embodying the wisdom and craftsmanship spirit of Chinese artisans. Furthermore, covered bridges have fostered a localized community culture due to their unique community functions. Covered bridges often serve as social gathering places where people seek shelter from the elements, rest, and converse, gradually evolving into trading markets for exchanging goods and services. Later, they even became venues for family banquets, weddings, funerals, and other events. Consequently, a community culture centered on covered bridges naturally emerged. With their profound historical and cultural heritage, exquisite appearance, and superb bridge-building techniques, China's covered bridges have elevated the covered bridge culture to new heights.

Learning from the past to predict the future, the creations of our ancestors have provided subtle cultural nourishment for future generations. China's covered bridges epitomize a solution devised by people to address the multifaceted relationships between humanity and nature, life and production, material and spiritual aspects, resources and the environment. They are not only invaluable material heritages left by ancient Chinese transport professionals who dared to build roads over mountains and bridges over rivers, but also invaluable spiritual treasures that we should inherit in the process of redoubling efforts to make China a country with great transport strength.

Editors
September 2024

目 录 CONTENTS

三国时期　The Three Kingdoms period

肖家山桥　Xiaojiashan Bridge ……………………… 003
龙潭桥　Longtan Bridge ……………………………… 004

隋唐　Sui and Tang Dynasties

桥楼殿　Qiaolou Temple ……………………………… 009
澄波桥　Chengbo Bridge ……………………………… 010
琉璃桥　Liuli Bridge …………………………………… 011
扣冰桥　Koubing Bridge ……………………………… 012
金凤桥　Jinfeng Bridge ………………………………… 013

宋代　Song Dynasty

观音阁桥　Guanyinge Bridge ………………………… 016
万福桥　Wanfu Bridge ………………………………… 017
花桥　Huaqiao Bridge ………………………………… 018
广福桥　Guangfu Bridge ……………………………… 019
熟溪桥　Shuxi Bridge ………………………………… 020
官局桥　Guanju Bridge ……………………………… 021
三条桥　Santiao Bridge ……………………………… 022

龙津桥　Longjin Bridge ……………………………… 023
矮殿桥　Aidian Bridge ………………………………… 024
普通桥　Putong Bridge ……………………………… 025
万安桥　Wan'an Bridge ……………………………… 027
沉字桥　Chenzi Bridge ……………………………… 028
千乘桥　Qiansheng Bridge …………………………… 029
龙井桥　Longjing Bridge ……………………………… 030
观音桥　Guanyin Bridge ……………………………… 031
百祥桥　Baixiang Bridge ……………………………… 032
通仙桥　Tongxian Bridge ……………………………… 033
瑞云桥　Ruiyun Bridge ……………………………… 034
登龙桥　Denglong Bridge ……………………………… 035
济美桥　Jimei Bridge ………………………………… 036
拱北桥　Gongbei Bridge ……………………………… 037
上大夫桥　Shangdafu Bridge ………………………… 038
彩虹桥　Caihong Bridge ……………………………… 040
登仙桥　Dengxian Bridge ……………………………… 042
梅岭桥　Meiling Bridge ……………………………… 043
古莲桥　Gulian Bridge ………………………………… 044
广济桥　Guangji Bridge ……………………………… 045
百梁桥　Bailiang Bridge ……………………………… 047
广济桥　Guangji Bridge ……………………………… 048

洪济桥　Hongji Bridge ·· 049

元代　Yuan Dynasty

灵润桥　Lingrun Bridge ····································· 052
半路亭桥　Banluting Bridge ································ 053
回龙桥　Huilong Bridge ····································· 054
仁寿桥　Renshou Bridge ···································· 055
环秀桥　Huanxiu Bridge ···································· 056
高阳桥　Gaoyang Bridge ···································· 057

明代　Ming Dynasty

仙桥　Xianqiao Bridge ·· 060
峦桥　Luanqiao Bridge ······································· 061
环翠桥　Huancui Bridge ····································· 063
断涧仙桥　Duanjian Xianqiao Bridge ·················· 064
灞陵桥　Baling Bridge ·· 065
龙凤桥　Longfeng Bridge ···································· 066
云龙桥　Yunlong Bridge ····································· 066
映月桥　Yingyue Bridge ····································· 067
太极桥　Taiji Bridge ·· 068

刘家桥　Liujia Bridge ·· 069
广济桥　Guangji Bridge ····································· 070
虹桥　Hongqiao Bridge ······································ 071
余庆桥　Yuqing Bridge ······································ 072
龙津桥　Longjin Bridge ····································· 073
万寿桥　Wanshou Bridge ···································· 074
人和桥　Renhe Bridge ······································· 074
迴澜桥　Huilan Bridge ······································ 075
青龙桥　Qinglong Bridge ···································· 076
普济桥　Puji Bridge ·· 077
佛殿桥　Fodian Bridge ······································ 078
宏济桥　Hongji Bridge ······································ 079
毓秀桥　Yuxiu Bridge ······································· 080
古溪桥　Guxi Bridge ··· 081
永和桥　Yonghe Bridge ······································ 082
兰溪桥　Lanxi Bridge ······································· 084
如龙桥　Rulong Bridge ······································ 085
步蟾桥　Buchan Bridge ····································· 086
白云桥　Baiyun Bridge ······································ 086
刘宅桥　Liuzhai Bridge ······································ 087
仙居桥　Xianju Bridge ······································ 088
薛宅桥　Xuezhai Bridge ····································· 089

登云桥	Dengyun Bridge	090
溪东桥	Xidong Bridge	091
飞云桥	Feiyun Bridge	092
三仙桥	Sanxian Bridge	093
老人桥	Laoren Bridge	094
金朱桥	Jinzhu Bridge	095
大宝桥	Dabao Bridge	096
金造桥	Jinzao Bridge	098
腾云桥	Tengyun Bridge	099
镇安桥	Zhen'an Bridge	100
五福桥	Wufu Bridge	103
花桥	Huaqiao Bridge	104
步月桥	Buyue Bridge	105
承安桥	Cheng'an Bridge	106
兴龙桥	Xinglong Bridge	107
集瑞桥	Jirui Bridge	108
永隆桥	Yonglong Bridge	109
云龙桥	Yunlong Bridge	110
见龙桥	Jianlong Bridge	111
神仙桥	Shenxian Bridge	112
流泗桥	Liusi Bridge	113
会清桥	Huiqing Bridge	114
广济桥	Guangji Bridge	116
乐寿桥	Leshou Bridge	117
云溪桥	Yunxi Bridge	118
三棵树桥	Sankeshu Bridge	119
通济桥	Tongji Bridge	121
泰新桥	Taixin Bridge	122
高桥	Gaoqiao Bridge	123
彩凤桥	Caifeng Bridge	125

清代　Qing Dynasty

水榭廊桥	Shuixie Covered Bridge	128
柳桥	Liuqiao Bridge	129
荇桥	Xingqiao Bridge	130
豳风桥	Binfeng Bridge	131
康庄桥	Kangzhuang Bridge	132
东河桥	Donghe Bridge	133
西河桥	Xihe Bridge	133
万寿桥	Wanshou Bridge	134
锡福桥	Xifu Bridge	135

回龙桥 Huilong Bridge	135
两河风雨桥 Lianghe Fengyu Bridge	136
马家滩桥 Majiatan Bridge	137
五星桥 Wuxing Bridge	138
烟雨廊桥 Yanyu Covered Bridge	139
接龙桥 Jielong Bridge	140
三曲桥 Sanqu Bridge	141
弥江桥 Mijiang Bridge	141
合益桥 Heyi Bridge	142
姊妹桥 Zimei Bridges	143
波日桥 Bori Bridge	145
虎啸桥 Huxiao Bridge	146
龙华凉桥 Longhua Liangqiao Bridge	146
保兴桥 Baoxing Bridge	147
永镇桥 Yongzhen Bridge	148
通京桥 Tongjing Bridge	149
天缘桥 Tianyuan Bridge	150
乡会桥 Xianghui Bridge	151
永顺桥 Yongshun Bridge	152
深溪河桥 Shenxihe Bridge	153
龙家桥 Longjia Bridge	154
永福桥 Yongfu Bridge	154
过路桥 Guolu Bridge	155
凉亭桥 Liangting Bridge	156
壶圆桥 Huyuan Bridge	157
长丰桥 Changfeng Bridge	158
肖家桥 Xiaojia Bridge	159
晏家桥 Yanjia Bridge	160
燕子桥 Yanzi Bridge	161
复古桥 Fugu Bridge	162
普修桥 Puxiu Bridge	163
廻龙桥 Huilong Bridge	163
普济桥 Puji Bridge	164
金勾风雨桥 Jingou Fengyu Bridge	165
地坪风雨桥 Diping Fengyu Bridge	166
牙双花桥 Yashuang Huaqiao Bridge	167
岑管花桥 Cenguan Huaqiao Bridge	168
翠谷桥 Cuigu Bridge	168
村尾花桥 Cunwei Huaqiao Bridge	169
巩福桥 Gongfu Bridge	170
邑团桥 Batuan Bridge	171
虹饮桥 Hongyin Bridge	172

东辕桥	Dongyuan Bridge	173
环涧桥	Huanjian Bridge	174
双溪桥	Shuangxi Bridge	174
钟灵桥	Zhongling Bridge	175
仁安桥	Ren'an Bridge	176
红军桥	Hongjun Bridge	177
通洲桥	Tongzhou Bridge	178
戈场桥	Gechang Bridge	179
慕义桥	Muyi Bridge	180
双溪桥	Shuangxi Bridge	181
黄水长桥	Huangshui Changqiao Bridge	182
护龙桥	Hulong Bridge	183
畲桥	Sheqiao Bridge	184
回龙桥	Huilong Bridge	184
环胜桥	Huansheng Bridge	185
护关桥	Huguan Bridge	186
大赤坑桥	Dachikeng Bridge	187
芎岱岭脚桥	Xiongdai Lingjiao Bridge	188
湖南亭桥	Hunan Tingqiao Bridge	189
北涧桥	Beijian Bridge	190
霞光桥	Xiaguang Bridge	191
永庆桥	Yongqing Bridge	192
普宾桥	Pubin Bridge	193
毓文桥	Yuwen Bridge	194
文兴桥	Wenxing Bridge	195
龙津桥	Longjin Bridge	196
赤岩虹桥	Chiyan Hongqiao Bridge	197
岭兜桥	Lingdou Bridge	197
升仙桥	Shengxian Bridge	198
馀庆桥	Yuqing Bridge	199
花桥	Huaqiao Bridge	200
乐丰桥	Lefeng Bridge	201
家坛桥	Jiatan Bridge	202
德胜桥	Desheng Bridge	202
种善桥	Zhongshan Bridge	203
后建桥	Houjian Bridge	204
高地桥	Gaodi Bridge	205
三溪桥	Sanxi Bridge	206
岭下桥	Lingxia Bridge	206
安仁桥	Anren Bridge	207
化龙桥	Hualong Bridge	208
玉沙桥	Yusha Bridge	208
蛟潭桥	Jiaotan Bridge	209
铭新桥	Mingxin Bridge	210

溪边桥	Xibian Bridge	211
宴林口桥	Yanlinkou Bridge	212
龙门桥	Longmen Bridge	213
麟清桥	Linqing Bridge	213
永镇桥	Yongzhen Bridge	214
韩家庄桥	Hanjiazhuang Bridge	215
永宁桥	Yongning Bridge	216
玉带桥	Yudai Bridge	217
初石桥	Chushi Bridge	218
永安桥	Yongan Bridge	219
太平桥	Taiping Bridge	220
三川桥	Sanchuan Bridge	221
万寿桥	Wanshou Bridge	222
玉带桥	Yudai Bridge	223
卧波桥	Wobo Bridge	224
逢源双桥	Fengyuan Shuangqiao Bridge	225
三亭桥	Santing Bridge	226
五亭桥	Wuting Bridge	227
后记	Epilogue	228

中 国 廊 桥 精 粹
The Quintessence of Covered Bridges in China

三国时期

220—280 年

　　东汉永平六年（63 年），陕西省勉县古褒城北石门溪谷阁道一侧凿刻的《开通褒斜道摩崖刻石》上写道："桥阁六百三十二间，大桥五，为道二百五十八里。"这是目前有关廊桥的最早文字记载，可惜没有廊桥实物遗留。在四川省以北的甘肃省文县，以南的云南省巍山彝族回族自治县，各发现的一座始建于三国时期的廊桥，是我国现存最古老的"桥阁"实物。桥址虽不在四川省，却与三国时期的蜀国政治、军事史以及而后"三国归晋"的历史事件有着重大关联。

The Three Kingdoms period
(220–280 AD)

In the sixth year of Yongping during the Eastern Han Dynasty (63 AD), the inscription on the *Kaitong Baoxiedao Moyakeshi*, located on one side of the Shimen Creek Valley near the ancient Baocheng in Mian County, Shaanxi Province, states: "There are 632 bridge pavilions, 5 large bridges, spanning a total of 258 *li* (during the Eastern Han Dynasty, 1 *li* was approximately equal to 415 meters)." This is currently the earliest written record of covered bridges, but unfortunately, no physical remnants of these bridges have been preserved. Presently, two covered bridges dating back to the Three Kingdoms period have been discovered in Wenxian County, Gansu Province, north of Sichuan Province, and in Weishan Yi and Hui Autonomous County, Yunnan Province, south of Sichuan Province. These bridges represent the oldest existing physical examples of "bridge pavilions" in China. Although the bridge sites are not located within Sichuan Province, they are significantly related to the political and military history of the Shu Kingdom during the Three Kingdoms period, as well as to the historical event of "the Three Kingdoms united by Jin Dynasty".

肖家山桥

甘肃省文县铁楼藏族乡肖家山村白马河,三国时期(220—280年)

始建于三国时期,历代修缮。石木结构叠木支撑平梁廊桥,长25米、宽2米、高5米,八开间,顶覆小青瓦,两端建有鹅卵石挡墙,并建凉亭式门楼。文县古称"阴平"。《三国志·魏书·邓艾传》曾记载:"冬十月,(邓)艾自阴平道,行无人之地七百余里,凿山通道,造作桥阁。山高谷深,至为艰险,又粮运将匮,频于危殆。艾以毡自裹,推转而下。将士皆攀木缘崖,鱼贯而进。"其中的"桥阁",正是廊桥的古称。

Xiaojiashan Bridge

over Baima River, Xiaojiashan Village, Tielou Tibetan Autonomous Township, Wenxian County, Gansu Province, built during 220-280 AD.

Xiaojiashan Bridge, was originally constructed buring 220-280 AD, and has undergone restoration in successive dynasties. The bridge is a stone and wood structure with a flat beam supported by laminated wood, measuring 25 meters in length, 2 meters in width, and 5 meters in height, with 8 bays. Its roof is covered with small grey tiles, and cobblestone retaining walls are built at both ends, along with a pavilion-style gate-tower. Wen County was historically known as "Yinping". The *Records of the Three Kingdoms* (*Wei Shu*, *Biography of Deng Ai*) notes: "In the winter of the tenth month, (Deng) Ai travelled over 700 *li* through uninhabited lands via the Yinping Road, cutting through mountains to create a path and constructing bridge pavilions. The mountains were high and the valleys deep, making the journey extremely treacherous, and as the supply of provisions neared depletion, the situation became precarious. Ai wrapped himself in felt and rolled down. The soldiers clung to trees and climbed along cliffs, advancing in single file." The term "bridge pavilion" (桥阁 in Chinese) in this context refers to what is now known as covered bridge.

龙潭桥

云南省巍山彝族回族自治县巍宝山文昌宫，三国时期（220—280 年）

龙潭桥又名文龙亭桥。文昌宫住持阁永仁道长（大理白族自治州道教协会副会长）介绍："寺观建于三国时代（220—280 年），龙潭桥也是那个时候建的。"由石台、木柱、飞檐翘角歇山顶组成水榭亭桥，具有云南大屋顶建筑风格。桥亭主脊较高，有朵梅、卷草装饰。四檐头各蹲"鱼化龙"兽吻一尊。桥亭顶部覆青色筒瓦，橡头置有图案各异的瓦当。柱头、横梁、斗拱、额枋均留有精美华丽彩绘。

Longtan Bridge

Wenchang Palace, Weibao Mountain, Weishan Yi and Hui Autonomous County, Yunnan Province, built during 220-280 AD.

Longtan Bridge, also known as the Wenlongting Bridge. Yan Yongren, Vice President of the Dali Bai Autonomous Prefecture Taoist Association, who presides over the Wenchang Palace-Temple, explained that the temple was built in the Three Kingdoms Period (220-280 AD), and Longtan Bridge was built then. This waterside pavilion bridge is composed of a stone platform, timber columns, and a hip and gable roof with upturned eaves at the corners. The large roof is characteristic of Yunnan style architecture. The main ridge of the bridge pavilion is high, decorated with assorted plum and scroll grass patterns. Each of the four eaves is decorated with fish-turning-into-dragon ornaments. The top of the bridge pavilion is covered with grey semi-circular tiles, and the ends of the rafters (called *wadang*) are carved with different patterns. The bridge's columns, crossbeams, dougong brackets, and plaques are all beautifully painted.

中 国 廊 桥 精 粹

The Quintessence of Covered Bridges in China

隋　唐

581—907 年

《中国古代桥梁》作者唐寰澄考证，现存最早的廊桥是隋代建造的河北井陉桥楼殿。唐太和五年（831年），白居易（772—846年，祖籍太原，现实主义诗人）用武昌军节度使元稹（779—831年，洛阳人，诗人、文学家，官至宰相，后遭贬）病危时托付的一笔银两，大修洛阳香山寺并撰写《修香山寺记》。《修香山寺记》中所提"始自寺前，亭一所，登寺桥一所，连桥廊七间"，不经意间记录了唐代廊桥的确凿信息。目前在中国境内发现的隋唐廊桥数量很少而且分散，有着弥足珍贵的历史文化价值。令人称奇的是，这些廊桥大部分仍在使用。

Sui and Tang Dynasties
(581–907 AD)

Tang Huancheng, the author of *Chinese Ancient Bridges*, has verified that the earliest existing covered bridge is Qiaolou Temple in Jingxing, Hebei Province, built during the Sui Dynasty (581-618 AD). In the fifth year of the Taihe reign of Emperor Wenzong of the Tang Dynasty (831 AD), the poet Bai Juyi (772-846 AD), a realist poet originally from Taiyuan, used funds entrusted to him by Yuan Zhen (779-831 AD), the *Jiedushi* (a title for regional military governors in China) of Wuchang and a poet and literary figure who later fell from prime minister and got demoted, to undertake extensive renovations of the Xiangshan Temple in Luoyang and composed the *Record of the Renovation of Xiangshan Temple*. In this record, he notes, "Starting from the front of the temple, there is a pavilion and a bridge leading to the temple, connecting seven bays of a covered bridge", inadvertently providing concrete evidence of the existence of covered bridges during the Tang Dynasty. Currently, the number of covered bridges built in Sui and Tang Dynasties discovered in China is quite limited and scattered, possessing invaluable historical and cultural significance. Remarkably, most of these covered bridges are still in use today.

桥楼殿

河北省井陉县苍岩山断崖，隋代（581—618年）

桥楼殿跨越苍岩山崖断裂，坐西向东，长15米、宽9米、跨径10.7米，地势奇险。清康熙（1662—1722年）年间，上部殿宇焚毁后复建。单跨敞肩拱桥，石缝以蝶形铁箍加固，九脊重檐回廊楼殿，歇山顶覆黄绿色琉璃瓦。奇特的创意、精巧的构造、非凡的技艺，在世界古代桥梁史上独一无二。古人赞叹"千丈虹桥望入微，天光云影共楼飞"。为全国重点文物保护单位。

Qiaolou Temple

Cangyan Mountain Cliff, Jingxing County, Hebei Province, built during 581-618 AD.

It runs in an east-west direction between the perilously steep cliffs of the Cangyan Mountain. The bridge is 15 meters long, 9 meters wide, and spans 10.7 meters. The terrain is extremely steef and treacherous. During the reign of Kangxi (1662-1722 AD) in the Qing Dynasty, the upper palace was reconstructed after burning down. It is a single-span open-shouldered stone arch bridge with butterfly-shaped iron fasteners as stone joints. Its gallery house is covered by a hip and gable roof with double eaves, nine roof ridges and yellow-green glazed tiles. The structure is exquisite and wonderful. This bridge is unique for its creativity and structure. There is no equivalent to it in the world's history of bridge building. In ancient times, it was praised with the lines, "The rainbow bridge reaches far into the distance and looks into the sky. It flies by the sun's rays and the clouds's shadows." It has been listed as a major historical and cultural sites protected at the national level.

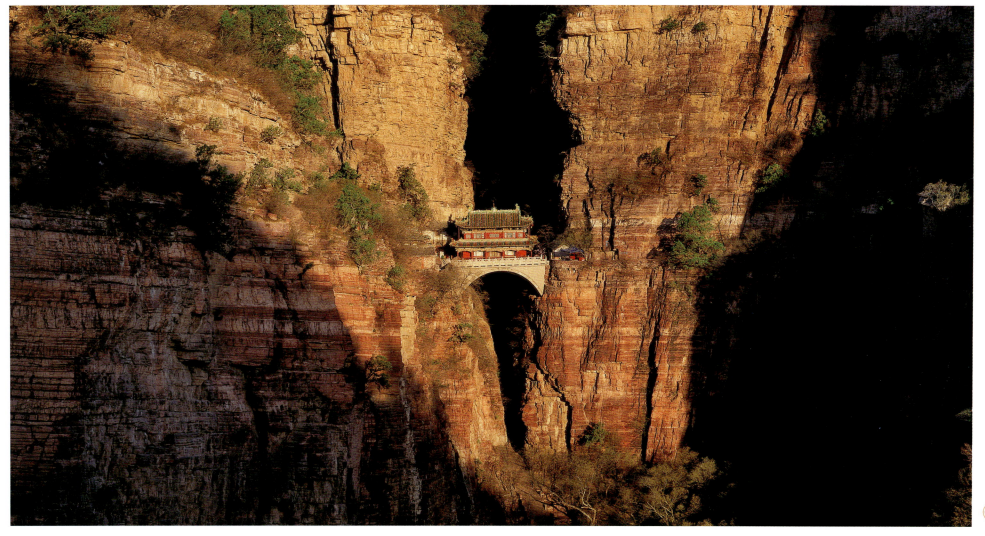

澄波桥

江西省铅山县湖坊镇陈坊河，唐贞观四年（630年）

唐代澄波和尚募捐，百姓协助兴建。该桥为石墩木平廊桥，长60余米、宽4米。桥头建有砖石门庭。门额镌刻"河清海晏""风静浪恬"，据传为澄波和尚墨迹。桥墩为尖锐船首型，墩尾平直，工匠称为"分水金刚墙"。石墩上纵横堆叠七层方形木枕，俗称"喜鹊窝"。两墩之间架设长大贯木主梁，全木结构。为省级文物保护单位。

Chengbo Bridge

over Chenfang River, Hufang Town, Yanshan County, Jiangxi Province, built in 630 AD.

During the Tang Dynasty, the monk Chengbo raised money to build this bridge with the help of local people. It is a simply supported covered bridge with stone piers, with a length of more than 60 meters and a width of 4 meters. A masonry gateway at the bridge head has a plaque inscribed with the words "Clear River and Tranquil Seas" and "Calm Winds and Still Waters", said to be written by monk Chengbo. One side of the pier is sharp like a ship bow, while the other side is flat. It is called "water-separating jingang wall" by carpenters. On top of the stone piers are seven criss-crossed layers of timber known as a "magpie nest". Between the piers is the large timber main beam connecting the complete timber structure. It has been listed as a historical and cultural sites protected at the provincial level.

琉璃桥

西藏自治区拉萨市大昭寺西街，唐贞观十九年（645年）

中国海拔最高的廊桥。藏语称"宇妥桑巴"，意为"绿松石桥"，被列为自治区重点文物保护单位。该桥为石木结构，跨径28.5米、宽6.8米，甬堂式桥廊，石墙厚1米，无立柱。有5个宽2.3~2.5米孔洞，间距2.6米，高3.2米，属汉藏结合建筑。四檐翘角上安有琉璃龙首，屋脊中央竖立高1米琉璃宝顶，两端设琉璃供果脊幢。河流上游改道后，"琉璃桥下琉璃水"已不复存在。

Liuli Bridge

West Street of Jokhang Temple, Lhasa, Tibet Autonomous Region, built in 645 AD.

This is the highest covered bridge in China. The Liuli Bridge is called "Yutuo Sangba" in Tibetan, meaning that it is a turquoise stone bridge. It is listed as a major historical and cultural sites protected at the level of Autonomous Region. The bridge is built of stone and timber. It is 28.5 meters long, 6.8 meters wide, the gallery walls are 1 meter thick, and there are no internal supporting columns. The five arches under the bridge are 2.3 to 2.5 meters wide, 3.2 meters high, and set 2.6 meters apart. The structure combines the characteristics of both Han and Tibetan architecture. There are glazed dragon heads on the upturned corners of the four eaves, and in the center of the roof ridge stands a one meter tall glazed treasure top. There are also glazed designs of fruit on both ends of the ridge. After the upper reaches of the river were diverted, "glazed water underneath the glazed bridge" has disappeared.

扣冰桥

福建省武夷山市吴屯乡瑞岩寺,唐广明元年(880年)

扣冰桥是与瑞岩寺同时代的建筑。据法悟师父介绍:"瑞岩寺是千年古寺,扣冰桥为千年古桥。扣冰桥始建于唐广明元年(880年),古代扣冰桥建有百米长廊,廊顶铺满黄色琉璃瓦。远远望去就像隐行在翠林中的一条黄龙。"今天的扣冰桥长30余米,廊顶上的琉璃瓦已被小青瓦取代。瑞岩寺及附属扣冰桥均为市级文物保护单位。

Koubing Bridge

Ruiyan Temple, Wutun Township, Wuyishan, Fujian Province, built in 880 AD.

Koubing Bridge was built about the same time as the Ruiyan Temple. According to monk Fawu, "Ruiyan Temple has a history of about one thousand years, and so does the bridge. Koubing Bridge was built in the first year of the Guangming period in the Tang Dynasty (880 AD). It had a gallery about one hundred meters long and was covered by yellow glazed tiles, resembling a yellow dragon cloaked by the surrounding green woods." Koubing Bridge is now 30 meters long and covered by small grey tiles. Ruiyan Temple and the bridge are both listed as a historical and cultural sites protected at the municipal level.

金凤桥

四川省邛崃市大同镇景沟村，唐代（618—907 年）

金凤桥横跨景沟河，一墩两孔，为石拱木屋廊桥，长 10 米、宽 3.3 米、高 3.5 米。两端各有六级台阶，并设置八个廊仓，寓意六六大顺、余粮满仓。两侧石拱中间上方安置龙首龙尾，寓意压水头护村保桥，金凤桥的古木青瓦飞檐翘角，深得村民喜爱。据桥碑记述："金凤桥始建于唐（代），初为茶马商贩渡河歇脚之用，兴盛于明清时，重建于民国二十四年（1935 年）。"为市级文物保护单位。

Jinfeng Bridge

Jinggou Village, Datong Town, Qionglai, Sichuan Province, built during 618-907 AD.

Jinfeng Bridge spans the Jinggou River with a single pier and two arches. It is a stone arch wooden covered bridge, measuring 10 meters in length, 3.3 meters in width, and 3.5 meters in height. Each end features six steps and eight storage compartments, symbolizing everything going smoothly and a bountiful harvest. Dragon heads and tails are placed above the stone arches on both sides, symbolizing protection for the village and the bridge. The bridge's ancient wooden structure and grey-tiled eaves are cherished by the villagers. According to the bridge inscription, "Jinfeng Bridge was originally built during the Tang Dynasty, initially serving as a rest stop for tea and horse traders crossing the river. It flourished during the Ming and Qing Dynasties and was rebuilt in 1935 AD." The bridge has been listed as a historical and cultural sites protected at the municipal level.

中 国 廊 桥 精 粹
The Quintessence of Covered Bridges in China

宋 代

960—1279 年

　　宋代是古代中国文化的繁盛时期，桥梁建筑工艺已经非常成熟，桥上常建有亭台楼阁。北宋画家王希孟在《千里江山图》中对廊桥有着细致生动的描绘，是整体画作的点睛之笔。江西省上饶市婺源县清华镇的彩虹桥（宋代建造）取自唐代诗人李白所写《秋登宣城谢朓北楼》一诗中"江城如画里，山晓望晴空。两水夹明镜，双桥落彩虹"的意境。彩虹桥是宋代廊桥的代表作。更为重要的是，中国廊桥建造师发明的穿插别压式木拱廊桥在浙南、闽北的山谷间开始规模化建设，这一划时代的桥梁支撑结构，被北宋天才画师张择端在《清明上河图》中完美呈现。

Song Dynasty

(960–1279 AD)

The Song Dynasty was a flourishing period in the culture of ancient China, during which bridge construction techniques became highly sophisticated, often featuring decorative pavilions and towers. The Northern Song painter Wang Ximeng provided a detailed and vivid depiction of covered bridges in his masterpiece *Thousand Miles of Rivers and Mountains*, which serves as a highlight of the overall composition. The Caihong Bridge (Rainbow Bridge) in Qinghua Town, Wuyuan County, Shangrao, Jiangxi Province, built during the Song Dynasty, draws inspiration from the poem *Climbing the Northern Tower of Xie Tiao in Xuancheng in the Autumn* by the Tang poet Li Bai, which includes the lines: "In the picturesque city by the river, the mountains greet the clear sky. Two waters embrace a bright mirror, while twin bridges arch like rainbows." The Caihong Bridge stands as a representative work of Song Dynasty covered bridges. Moreover, the invention of the interlocking and compressed wooden arch covered bridge by Chinese bridge builders marked the beginning of large-scale construction in the valleys of southern Zhejiang and northern Fujian. This groundbreaking structural innovation was perfectly depicted by the Northern Song genius artist Zhang Zeduan in his work *Along the River During the Qingming Festival*.

观音阁桥

湖南省宜章县笆篱镇才口村，北宋（960—1127年）

观音阁桥始建于北宋（960—1127年）时期。桥东端紧邻观音阁，为一墩两孔砖柱瓦顶三级宝塔式廊桥。三级宝塔用于纪念建寺的高僧和历代住持。观音阁桥保存完好，仍在造福当地的百姓。

Guanyinge Bridge

Caikou Village, Bali Town, Yizhang County, Hunan Province, built during 960-1127 AD.

Guanyinge Bridge was first built during the Northern Song Dynasty (960-1127 AD). The Guanyin Pavilion locates next to the east end of the covered bridge. The bridge forms the housing for a three-story pagoda with one pier and two spans. The bridge's internal columns are built of bricks, and the gallery house is covered with tiles. The three-story pagoda is used to commemorate the eminent monks who built the temple and the successive abbots. The Guanyinge Bridge is well preserved and still benefits local people.

万福桥

重庆市荣昌区铜鼓镇，南宋（1127—1279 年）

明万历（1573—1620 年）年间、清代（1644—1911 年）修缮。万福桥又称风雨廊桥，是重庆市年代最久远的古代廊桥。长 13 米、宽 5.7 米，圆木抬梁结构，硬山顶覆小青瓦，极具历史艺术价值。

Wanfu Bridge

Tonggu Town, Rongchang District, Chongqing, built during 1127-1279 AD.

During the reign of Wanli in the Ming Dynasty (1573-1620 AD) and the Qing Dynasty (1644-1911 AD), the bridge was renovated. Wanfu Bridge, also known as the Fengyu Covered Bridge, is the oldest ancient covered bridge in Chongqing. It is 13 meters long and 5.7 meters wide, with a round log cantilever structure, and the gable roof is covered with small grey tiles, which is of great historical and artistic value.

中国廊桥精粹

花桥

广西壮族自治区桂林市七星岩，南宋嘉熙（1237—1240年）

始建于南宋嘉熙（1237—1240年）年间，原名嘉熙桥，明代改名为花桥，清代改名为天柱桥。四墩五孔石拱敞廊式廊桥，元末明初水毁。明景泰七年（1456年），知府何永全集资在原址建石墩木桥。明嘉靖十九年（1540年）重修并增建旱桥五墩六孔，自此该桥由东西两段组成。东段水桥长60米，建有单脊双坡顶廊屋，十五开间，西段旱桥长65.2米，两段宽均为6.3米。1965年整修。

Huaqiao Bridge

Qixing Rock, Guilin, Guangxi Zhuang Autonomous Region, built during 1237-1240 AD.

The bridge was built during the Jiaxi period of the Song Dynasty (1237-1240 AD); it was originally called Jiaxi Bridge. Its name was then changed to Huaqiao Bridge in the Ming Dynasty and to Tianzhu Bridge in the Qing Dynasty. It is a stone arch and open gallery type covered bridge with four piers and five spans. Between the late Yuan and early Ming Dynasties, it was destroyed by flood. In 1456 AD, *zhifu* (the prefectural magistrate) He Yongquan collected funds to construct a timber bridge with stone piers at the original site of the bridge. In 1540 AD, the bridge was rebuilt, with the addition of a section over dry land with five piers and six spans, creating a complete bridge running from east to west with two sections. The east section passes over water and is 60 meters long. Its gallery house has 15 bays covered by a double sloping single ridge roof. The west section passes over dry land and is 65.2 meters long, and the whole bridge is 6.3 meters wide. It was renovated in 1965.

广福桥

广西壮族自治区全州县龙水镇光田村双车自然村，宋代（960—1279年）

现桥建于清嘉庆（1796—1820年）年间，为一墩两孔石平梁廊桥，长8米、宽3.6米、高5米，两间半开间，双坡顶连接马头墙山字门，四根石柱支撑廊顶。为县级文物保护单位。

Guangfu Bridge

Shuangche Natural Village, Guangtian Village, Longshui Town, Quanzhou County, Guangxi Zhuang Autonomous Region, built during 960-1279 AD.

The present bridge was built between 1796-1820 AD. It has one pier and two spans and is a stone flat beam supported bridge. It is 8 meters long, 3.6 meters wide, and 5 meters high. It has a gallery house with two and a half bays. Its double sloped roof is supported by four columns and is connected to the gate's horsehead wall. The bridge has been listed as a historical and cultural sites protected at the county level.

熟溪桥

浙江省武义县熟溪，南宋开禧三年（1207年）

原名石公桥，长140米、宽4.8米、高13.4米，八墩九孔，四十九开间，廊内设置木凳，中部建歇山顶亭阁。桥碑记："宋开禧三年（1207年），县主簿石宗玉发起修筑，称石公桥。700多年间，熟溪桥屡建屡毁。明嘉靖二十五年（1546年）建六墩，明万历四年（1576年）增至十墩。桥长五十丈、宽一丈七尺，并建桥屋四十九间。清乾隆四十九年（1784年）重修桥屋至五十一间，两侧卫以护栏。"为省级文物保护单位。

Shuxi Bridge

Shuxi Creek, Wuyi County, Zhejiang Province, built in 1207 AD.

Shuxi Bridge, formerly known as Shigong Bridge, is 140 meters long, 4.8 meters wide, and 13.4 meters high. It has eight piers and nine spans. Its gallery house has 49 bays, and timber benches run along its length. A pavilion with a hip and gable roof is built in its middle. A stele by the bridge states, "Shi Zongyu, the county's *zhubu* (secretary of the magistrate), initiated the construction of Shigong Bridge in 1207 AD. Over the past 700 years, the bridge has been built and destroyed repeatedly. Six piers were built in 1546 AD, then four more in 1576 AD, at which time the bridge was 50 *zhang* long and 1 *zhang* and 7 *chi* wide. During this time, a gallery house with 49 bays was built on the bridge as well. In 1784 AD, the gallery house was rebuilt with 51 bays, and protective railing was added to both sides." The bridge has been listed as a historical and cultural sites protected at the provincial level.

官局桥

浙江省庆元县岭头乡，南宋绍兴二十八年（1158 年）

官局桥连通浙江省丽水市庆元县至福建省宁德市寿宁县之间的古官道，长 11.8 米、宽 4.15 米、高 3.8 米，单孔跨径 2.9 米。现如今，官局桥已不再当作桥梁使用，专供种田劳作的乡民及耕牛躲避风雨。

Guanju Bridge

Lingtou Township, Qingyuan County, Zhejiang Province, built in 1158 AD.

Guanju Bridge connects the ancient official road from Qingyuan County, Lishui, Zhejiang Province, to Shouning County, Ningde, Fujian Province. It is 11.8 meters long, 4.15 meters wide, and 3.8 meters high, with a single-span arch of 2.9 meters. Today, Guanju Bridge is no longer used as a bridge but serves as a shelter for local farmers and their oxen from the wind and rain.

三条桥

浙江省泰顺县罗阳镇洲岭社区，宋代（960—1279 年）

三条桥最初用三根粗大圆木搭建，因而得名。据泰顺县志记述，修缮三条桥时发现顶瓦中尚存刻有唐"贞观"文字的旧瓦。专家据此推断三条桥可能建于唐代贞观（627—649 年）年间。该桥为伸臂式全木结构廊桥，长 32 米、宽 4.9 米、高 12.6 米、跨径 21.3 米，十一开间。南宋绍兴七年（1137 年）、清道光二十三年（1843 年）重建。属于泰顺廊桥，为全国重点文物保护单位。

Santiao Bridge

Zhouling Community, Luoyang Town, Taishun County, Zhejiang Province, built during 960-1279 AD.

The bridge was initially built out of three thick logs, from which its name is derived. According to the Taishun County Annals, tiles engraved with the characters for "Zhenguan" were found while repairing the Santiao Bridge. As a result, experts inferred that the Santiao Bridge was built in the Zhenguan period of the Tang Dynasty (627-649 AD). Now it is a timber cantilever beam covered bridge. The bridge is 32 meters long, 4.9 meters wide, 12.6 meters high, and has a span of 21.3 meters. Its gallery house has 11 bays. The bridge was reconstructed in 1137 AD and in 1843 AD. Santiao Bridge is classified as Taishun Covered Bridges, which have been listed as a major historical and cultural sites protected at the national level.

龙津桥

福建省闽侯县廷坪乡流源村，宋代（960—1279年）

始建于宋代，明崇祯四年（1631年）改建为伸臂式木拱廊桥，桥长33米、宽4.3米。清乾隆二十年（1755年）、清道光二十三年（1843年）重修。桥面距河床高达30余米。

Longjin Bridge

Liuyuan Village, Tingping Township, Minhou County, Fujian Province, built during 960-1279 AD.

Longjin Bridge was originally constructed during the Song Dynasty (960-1279 AD) and was modified into a cantilevered wooden arch covered bridge in 1631 AD. It is 33 meters long and 4.3 meters wide. The bridge underwent significant repairs in 1755 AD and 1843 AD. The bridge deck stands more than 30 meters above the riverbed.

矮殿桥

福建省政和县杨源乡杨源村,北宋崇宁(1102—1106年)

又名杨源水尾桥、朝阳桥。南北走向,单孔平梁全木廊桥,长19.5米、宽6.5米、高8.3米、跨径10.8米,七开间。飞檐翘角重檐歇山顶覆小青瓦,八角覆斗藻井描绘《西游记》《三国演义》故事。廊屋为穿斗式结构,以榫卯连接,中部神龛供奉观世音菩萨,北端设三层塔式香纸炉,两侧铺钉,双层风雨板,下置木凳。1929年重修。

Aidian Bridge

Yangyuan Village, Yangyuan Township, Zhenghe County, Fujian Province, built during 1102-1106 AD.

Also known as Yangyuan Shuiwei Bridge or Chaoyang Bridge. The bridge runs from north to south and is a timber frame covered bridge with a single span. It is 19.5 meters long, 6.5 meters wide, 8.3 meters high, and has a span of 10.8 meters. It has a gallery house with 7 bays. The eaves and cornices on the top of the hip and gable roof are covered with small grey tiles, and its eight-panel caisson *zaojing* ceiling depicts scenes from the Chinese classics *Journey to the West* and *Romance of the Three Kingdoms*. The gallery house is a *chuandou* style structure and is connected by mortise and tenon technology. The central shrine is dedicated to Guanyin, the Buddhist bodhisattva of compassion. At the north side of the bridge is a three-story pagoda-style oven for burning incense and paper. There are timber benches under the double-layer wind and rain awnings on both sides of the bridge. The bridge was rebuilt in 1929 AD.

普通桥

福建省建瓯市小桥镇，南宋（1127—1279年）

一墩两孔木拱廊桥，长60米、宽5米、高9米。桥墩由当地山石料砌筑，两端建有门亭。双层挡雨木板之间设置木栅廊窗，单脊双坡顶覆小青瓦。

Putong Bridge

Xiaoqiao Town, Jian'ou, Fujian Province, built during 1127-1279 AD.

The bridge has one pier and two spans. It is a timber arch covered bridge that is 60 meters long, 5 meters wide, and 9 meters high. The piers are made of stones from local mountains, and there is a gateway pavilion at each end of the bridge. Timber lattices between the two layers of rain awnings at the sides of the bridge serve as windows for the gallery house. The single ridge two-slope roof is covered with small grey tiles.

万安桥

福建省屏南县长桥镇，北宋元祐五年（1090 年）

  又名长桥、龙江公桥。五墩六孔不等跨木拱廊桥，长 98.2 米、宽 4.7 米、高 8.5 米，三十八开间，九檩穿斗式构架，双坡单檐悬山顶。明万历二年（1574 年），山贼为阻断追剿，将万安桥烧毁，清乾隆七年（1742 年）重建。清道光二十五年（1845 年）乡绅筹资重建。该桥于中华民国初年因流民取暖失火焚毁，1932 年重建。属于闽东北廊桥，为全国重点文物保护单位。2022 年 8 月 6 日焚毁，2024 年 1 月 21 日修复。

Wan'an Bridge

Changqiao Town, Pingnan County, Fujian Province, built in 1090 AD.

It is also known as Changqiao Bridge and Longjianggong Bridge. It is a timber arch covered bridge with five piers. Its six spans are of different respective lengths. It is 98.2 meters long, 4.7 meters wide, and 8.5 meters high. Its gallery house is a *chuandou* structure with 38 bays and nine purlins. It is covered by a two-sloped overhanging gable roof with a single eave. In 1574 AD, bandits burned the Wan'an Bridge down in order to avoid their pursuers. The bridge was rebuilt in 1742 AD. In 1845 AD, local gentry raised funds for its reconstruction. In the early years of the Republic of China, refugees burned it down accidentally while trying to stay warm from the cold. The bridge was rebuilt again in 1932 AD. Wan'an Bridge is classified as the Covered Bridges in the east and north of Fujian, which have been listed as a major historical and cultural sites protected at the national level. The bridge was burned down on August 6, 2022 and repaired on January 21, 2024.

沉字桥

福建省古田县鹤塘镇西洋村，南宋德祐元年（1275年）

民谚传说，"宋中期溪岭十岁男孩'谢神童'路过新建廊桥，在桥柱题写对联'中国有至仁书同文车同轨，圣人必得寿月重轮星重晖'。人们琢磨之际墨迹已入木三分，定名沉字桥。"四墩五孔石墩木梁廊桥，船首式石墩，抬梁式全木结构，内设木凳、木栏，单檐庑殿顶覆青杂瓦。长54米、宽3.8米、高5.8米，十七开间。该桥连接古田与宁德驿道，为县级文物保护单位。

Chenzi Bridge

Xiyang Village, Hetang Town, Gutian County, Fujian Province, built in 1275 AD.

As a local folk tale goes, "In the middle of the Song Dynasty, there was a ten-year-old boy known as Prodigy Xie. He came across a newly built bridge and wrote a couplet on its columns. The ink words penetrated deep into the logs before anyone could figure out their meaning, so the bridge was named Chenzi Bridge." The bridge has four piers and five spans. Its piers are made of stone, and its beams of wood. Its piers are shaped in the forms of the bows of ships. The gallery house is a *tailiang* style structure with 17 bays. The bridge is 54 meters long, 3.8 meters wide, and 5.8 meters high. Inside the bridge there are timber benches and railings. It is covered by a single-eave hip roof and topped with assorted grey tiles. The bridge is located along the ancient courier road that connected Gutian to Ningde. It has been listed as a historical and cultural sites protected at the county level.

千乘桥

福建省屏南县棠口镇，宋代（960—1279 年）

又名祥峰桥。南北走向，石墩木拱廊桥，长 62.8 米、宽 5 米，二十二开间，一墩两孔，跨径各 27.5 米。九檩穿斗式构架，两侧安置木凳，飞檐翘角悬山顶覆小青瓦。桥南端遗存三方功德碑，其中一方《千乘桥志》记载："棠溪有桥颜曰千乘，双峰其对峙也，双涧汇其流也。虽居僻壤而北抵县城，南通省郡实往来之通衢。自宋以来重建三次矣。"

Qiansheng Bridge

Tangkou Town, Pingnan County, Fujian Province, built during 960-1279 AD.

Also known as Xiangfeng Bridge. This is a timber arch covered bridge with one stone pier and two spans. It runs from north to south and is 62.8 meters long, 5 meters wide, and each span 27.5 meters. Its gallery house has 22 bays. Timber benches are placed on both sides of the bridge house, which has nine purlins and is a *chuandou* style structure. Small grey tiles cover the hip and gable roof with upturned eaves. At the southern end of the bridge, there is a three stele extolling acts of merit and virtue. On one stele, the *Record of Qiansheng Bridge* states that, "The Tang Creek's bridge was called Qiansheng Bridge, its two peaks confronted each other, and two streams converged into one another. Although situated in a remote area to the north of which is the county seat, the south is connected with neighboring provinces, and hence it is a thoroughfare for coming and going. It has been rebuilt three times since the Song Dynasty (960-1279 AD)."

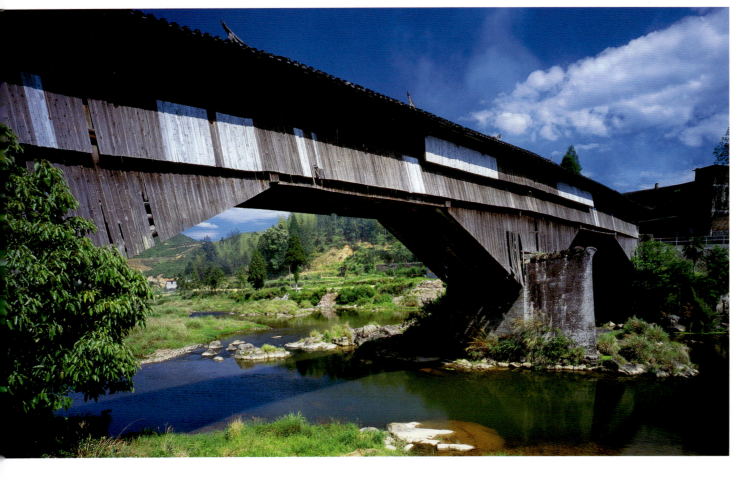

龙井桥

福建省屏南县寿山乡白玉村金造溪峡口,宋代（960—1279年）

清乾隆（1736—1795年）年间焚毁,清嘉庆二十五年（1820年）重建,清光绪十四年（1888年）修缮。全木结构伸臂式木拱廊桥,长27.5米、宽4.9米、跨径22.2米,十三开间,九檩穿斗式构架,单脊挑檐悬山顶。为县级文物保护单位。

Longjing Bridge

The Narrows of the Jinzao Creek, Baiyu Village, Shoushan Township, Pingnan County, Fujian Province, built during 960-1279 AD.

It burned during the reign of Qianlong (1736-1795 AD) in the Qing Dynasty and was rebuilt in 1820 AD. It was repaired in 1888 AD. It is a timber frame cantilever arch bridge, 27.5 meters long, 4.9 meters wide, and with a span of 22.2 meters. Its gallery house has 13 bays and is a *chuandou* style structure with nine purlins supporting an overhanging gable roof with a single ridge and extended eaves. It has been listed as a historical and cultural sites protected at the county level.

观音桥

福建省周宁县浦源镇浦源村鲤鱼溪，宋代（960—1279 年）

圆木平梁木结构廊桥，长 8 米、宽 4 米、高 5 米，东西走向，两侧设置木墙，南面开窗，双层挑檐悬山顶覆小青瓦，顶脊有两条奔龙和鱼化龙雕像，西端紧靠郑氏祠堂。桥梁与寺庙合一，供奉观世音菩萨。浦源村逢年过节、逢喜庆大事，都会往溪中放生鲤鱼，久而久之蜿蜒一华里鲤鱼满溪。村民爱鱼、护鱼、敬鱼，迷恋于鲤鱼的美丽与自由、健康与优雅，而他们自己又何尝不是如此呢？

Guanyin Bridge

Liyu Creek, Puyuan Village, Puyuan Town, Zhouning County, Fujian Province, built during 960-1279 AD.

This timber log beam covered bridge stretches from east to west and is 8 meters long, 4 meters wide, and 5 meters high. A timber wall is built on both of its sides, and a window faces out from its south. The gallery house is covered by a double-layer overhanging gable roof, covered by small grey tiles. The roof ridge is decorated by figures of a running dragon, and of a fish transforming into a dragon. The west end is close to the ancestral hall of the Zheng family. This combined bridge and temple is used to worship Guanyin, the Buddhist bodhisattva of compassion. Villagers from throughout Puyuan release carp in the stream on festivals, wishing the river to be full of carp long into the future. Residents here love, protect, and respect fish. They are fascinated by the beauty, freedom, health, and elegance of carp, attributes that probably can be ascribed to themselves as well.

百祥桥

福建省屏南县棠口镇山棠村下坑尾自然村与寿山乡太保村白洋自然村交界白洋溪，南宋咸淳（1265—1274年）

又名松柏桥、白洋桥，在历史上是闽北地区贯通西部山区与东部沿海"茶盐古道"重要节点。独孔全木结构伸臂式木拱廊桥，长38米、宽4.5米、跨径35米，桥面距谷底27米。四柱九檩穿斗式桥廊。清道光（1821—1850年）、咸丰（1851—1861年）年间重建。清光绪（1875—1908年）年间重修后，漈头、旺坑村十余人合资买下桥西一片山坡，植杉树480余株作为修桥专用林。同时捐谷放贷，收取薄利作为每年立冬村民锄草扫桥的午餐。屏南县的百祥桥、千乘桥、万安桥，均被列为全国重点文物保护单位，有"百千万"之名。

Baixiang Bridge

Baiyang Creek at the junction of Baiyang Natural Village in Shoushan Township and Xiakenwei Natural Village in Tangkou Town, Pingnan County, Fujian Province, built during 1265-1274 AD.

Also known as Songbai Bridge and Baiyang Bridge. Historically, this was an important node on the ancient "Tea and Salt Road" that linked the western mountainous areas to the eastern coastal areas in northern Fujian. It is a timber cantilever arch bridge with a single span. It is 38 meters long, 4.5 meters wide, and has a span of 35 meters. It sits 27 meters above the valley below. It has a *chuandou* style structure gallery house with four columns and nine purlins. It was reconstructed twice during the Daoguang (1821-1850 AD) and Xianfeng (1851-1861 AD) period in the Qing Dynasty. After its reconstruction during the Guangxu (1875-1908 AD) period in the Qing Dynasty, more than ten people from Jitou and Wangkeng villages jointly bought a hillside to the west of the Baixiang Bridge and planted more than 480 fir trees there to supply timber for the bridge's reconstruction. At the same time they donated grain and funds, and what was left was used annually for a lunch that villagers eat together on the bridge after completing weeding during the *lidong* period of the lunar calendar. Pingnan County's Baixiang Bridge, Qiansheng Bridge, and Wan'an Bridge are listed as a major historical and cultural sites protected at the national level and are referred to collectively by the first characters in their names—Bai Qian Wan, a homonym for "millions and millions".

通仙桥

福建省永春县东关镇东美村湖洋溪,南宋绍兴十五年(1145年)

原名东关桥,是闽南大型石墩木梁廊桥。长85米、宽5米,四墩五孔。清末遭暴雨重创破损,清光绪元年(1875年)复建。1929年,李俊承(1888—1966年,福建省永春县人,实业家,爱国华侨)出资,选取良材并招募能工巧匠,按宋代原貌重修。为省级文物保护单位,载入《中国名胜词典》。

Tongxian Bridge

Huyang Creek, Dongmei Village, Dongguan Town, Yongchun County, Fujian Province, built in 1145 AD.

Originally known as Dongguan Bridge, it is an example of a large-scale southern Fujian style stone pier timber beam covered bridge. It has four piers and five spans and is 85 meters long and 5 meters wide. It was damaged during the late Qing Dynasty, and was rebuilt in 1875 AD. In 1929 AD, Li Juncheng (1888-1966 AD), an overseas Chinese businessman and patriot, donated funds, found good quality materials, and recruited talented craftsmen to renovate the bridge to its original Song Dynasty look. It has been listed as a historical and cultural sites protected at the provincial level. It also is listed in the *Chinese Dictionary of Scenic Spots*.

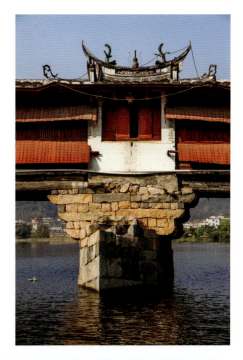

瑞云桥

福建省安溪县蓝田乡进德村进德溪，南宋咸淳元年（1265年）

　　该桥始建后两百年间遭遇两次水毁，皆获重建。明永乐三年（1405年）第三次水毁，当年秋按照高僧选定的吉日吉时，秉承九为尊祖制，精选9根长16米的粗壮杉木，砌筑桥堍，架木为梁，重建瑞云桥。明崇祯三年（1630年）整修。2007年焚毁，2008年重建。长14.7米、宽5米，桥廊内木雕精美。为县级文物保护单位。明代书法家张瑞图（1570—1644年，福建省晋江人）为瑞云桥书写"津梁大千"题匾。

Ruiyun Bridge

Jinde Creek, Jinde Village, Lantian Township, Anxi County, Fujian Province, built in 1265 AD.

In its first 200 years of existence, the bridge was rebuilt twice after being destroyed by floods. In the autumn of 1405 AD, after suffering damage caused by floods for a third time, the bridge was reconstructed with nine thick, 16-meter-long China firs on an auspicious date picked by a monk. It was renovated in 1630 AD. In 2007, it burned down and was rebuilt the following year. The bridge is 14.7 meters long and 5 meters wide, with exquisite wooden carvings inside its gallery house. It is listed as a historical and cultural sites protected at the county level. The words "Beams of Boundless Strength", written in the calligraphy of Zhang Ruitu, a native of Jinjiang, Fujian, who lived from 1570-1644 AD, grace a plaque that hangs from the bridge.

登龙桥

福建省德化县浔中镇蒲坂村，宋代（960—1279年）

曾名惠政桥、观音桥，连通德化县城通往大田县、尤溪县官道。两墩三孔，杉木搭跨为梁，全木结构，廊桥长62.5米、宽4.1米、高6.6米，十四开间。船首式桥墩，桥面铺杉木板，廊屋两侧安置条凳，外侧设木质双层雨披，硬山顶覆小青瓦。清顺治（1644—1661年）、康熙（1662—1722年）、雍正（1723—1735年）、乾隆（1736—1795年）、光绪（1875—1908年）年间整修。1923年，当地归国华侨陈簪发、李书植出资并发动海外华侨捐资9500银元，按古貌重建。为县级文物保护单位。

Denglong Bridge

Puban Village, Xunzhong Town, Dehua County, Fujian Province, built during 960-1279 AD.

Formerly called Huizheng Bridge and Guanyin Bridge, this bridge once connected the official road that linked Dehua's county seat to Datian and Youxi counties. The bridge has two piers and three spans. It is a timber beam covered bridge built with China fir. It is 62.5 meters long, 4.1 meters wide, 6.6 meters high, and rests on piers shaped in the form of ship bows. Its gallery house has 14 bays. The bridge road is covered with timber planks and benches are set on both of its sides. It has a flush gable roof, and the surfaces below are protected from the rain by two-layer awnings. The bridge was renovated during the Shunzhi (1644-1661 AD), Kangxi (1662-1722 AD), Yongzheng (1723-1735 AD), Qianlong (1736-1795 AD), and Guangxu (1875-1908 AD) periods of the Qing Dynasty. In 1923 AD, Chen Zanfa and Li Shuzhi, overseas Chinese residents originally from the area, returned home and organized other members of the overseas Chinese community to raise money for the bridge. They raised 9,500 silver dollars, with which the bridge was restored according to its original appearance. The bridge has been listed as a historical and cultural sites protected at the county level.

济美桥

福建省德化县水口镇承泽村石牛山,南宋（1127—1279年）

又名承泽桥。明万历（1573—1620年）、清乾隆（1736—1795年）年间修缮加固，1912—1949年间、1955年、1962年整修。承泽村黄氏族谱记载："亭桥建于南宋，位于乡之关键，悬崖飞瀑漈尾也。"圆木平梁廊桥，长22.5米、宽3.6米、高6米。桥基紧附山岩，基座由四层圆木分两组纵横叠搭支撑桥身。主梁中段有两根木柱作为辅助支撑，两侧安装木质雨披护板。

Jimei Bridge

Shiniu Mountain, Chengze Village, Shuikou Town, Dehua County, Fujian Province, built during 1127-1279 AD.

Also known as Chengze Bridge, this bridge was overhauled in the Wanli (1573-1620 AD) period of the Ming Dynasty, and during the Qianlong (1736-1795 AD) period of the Qing Dynasty. It was also repaired between 1912-1949 AD, 1955 and 1962. The Huang lineage genealogy in Chengze Village states that a pavilion bridge was built in the Southern Song Dynasty (1127-1279 AD) that served as a key connection for the area, and that it spanned over a waterfall. The current bridge is a timber horizontal log beam covered bridge. It is 22.5 meters long, 3.6 meters wide, and 6 meters high. The bridge foundation sits adjacent to the mountain's rock face. It uses four layers of logs, divided into two criss-crossing groups, to support the bridge body. There are two timber columns attached to the middle of the bridge's main beam that serve as a source of auxiliary support. Skirts to keep away the rain run along the length of the bridge.

拱北桥

安徽省休宁县蓝田镇迪岭村夹溪河,宋代(960—1279年)

拱北桥始建于宋代(960—1279年),明万历(1573—1620年)、清乾隆(1736—1795年)年间重建,桥上建有遮风避雨的砖木结构长廊,廊屋内设有靠背长条凳,是安徽省最长的古廊桥。拱北桥为徽派建筑风格的石墩木平廊桥,长75米、宽5米、高7.6米、四墩五孔。为省级文物保护单位。

Gongbei Bridge

Jiaxi River, Diling Village, Lantian Town, Xiuning County, Anhui Province, built during 960-1279 AD.

The Gongbei Bridge was built in the Song Dynasty (960-1279 AD) and was rebuilt in the Wanli (1573-1620 AD) period of the Ming Dynasty and the Qianlong (1736-1795 AD) period of the Qing Dynasty. Its gallery house is made of brick and wood. It has awnings on top to protect against the rain and benches with backrests installed inside. It is Anhui's longest ancient covered bridge. It has stone piers and timber beams and is built in the Huizhou architectural style. The bridge has four piers and five spans, and is 75 meters long, 5 meters wide, and 7.6 meters high. It has been listed as a historical and cultural sites protected at the provincial level.

上大夫桥

江西省婺源县沱川乡河西村篁村自然村，南宋（1127—1279年）

篁村原有两座南宋（1127—1279年）时期的廊桥，"大夫双桥"是为了纪念当地在宋代出了"双进士"而修建，均为木平梁结构，目前仅存一座。上大夫桥地处水口，长20米，桥面、桥柱、桥顶均为木质结构，廊屋两侧设靠背木椅，青瓦素墙木栏杆，马头墙桥口。

Shangdafu Bridge

Huangcun Natural Village, Hexi Village, Tuochuan Township, Wuyuan County, Jiangxi Province, built during 1127-1279 AD.

This village originally had two covered bridges built in the Southern Song Dynasty (1127-1279 AD) to commemorate two scholars who earned top rank in the imperial exams. They both were simply supported timber beam bridges, but only one remains. It is located at the village's water gap. It is 20 meters long, and its deck, columns, and roof are all made of wood material. Both sides of the bridge have wooden chairs and timber railings, and the gallery house is covered by grey tiles. There are horse-head walls at both ends of the bridge.

宋代 960—1279年

彩虹桥

江西省婺源县清华镇，南宋（1127—1279年）

　　南宋僧人胡济祥三年募集桥资，四年建成廊桥。覆盖最后几片青瓦时天空惊现彩虹，借"两水夹明镜，双桥落彩虹"之意定桥名。石墩木梁，长140米，宽3米，六亭五廊桥体桥墩不等距，船首船尾形制。廊亭、桥墩一体建造，构成抗击洪水冲压的独立体系。部分桥体毁损，整桥不必大拆大建。构件不用昂贵木料，梁栋不做雕刻彩绘，只为降低修复成本。维修不必聘请高级匠师，村里木匠即可胜任。2020年7月8日，部分桥面被洪水冲毁，2021年4月修复。

Caihong Bridge

Qinghua Town, Wuyuan County, Jiangxi Province, built during 1127-1279 AD.

Hu Jixiang, a Southern Song Dynasty monk, raised funds for the construction of the bridge in three years. The bridge was then constructed in four years. As the last few grey tiles were being installed, a rainbow suddenly appeared in the sky. He used a verse from the poet Li Bai, "two clear mirror rivers encircle, two bridges arched like rainbows above them" to give the bridge its name. The bridge has stone piers and timber beams. It is 140 meters long and 3 meters wide. It has six pavilions and five gallery structures. The bridge piers are separated by varying distances, and they are shaped like the bow and stern of a ship. The bridge pavilions and piers are built according to an independent flood resistant system. If a portion is destroyed, the entire bridge does not have to collapse. The components do not use expensive wood material, and beams are not carved or painted in order to reduce repair costs. As a result, there is no need to hire a senior craftsman for repairs, and village carpenters can complete any necessary work. On July 8, 2020, part of the bridge deck was destroyed by floods and was repaired in April 2021.

宋代 960—1279年

登仙桥

江西省乐安县谷岗乡登仙桥村，北宋开宝（968—976年）

该桥处地势险要，自古兵家必争，桥身弹痕累累。细长峡谷常有大雾，埋伏千军万马不易察觉。1933年，红一方面军在登仙桥反击第四次"围剿"，激战数小时活捉敌军师长、参谋长、旅长各一名，缴获武器一批、大洋数万元，史称"黄陂大捷"。硝烟散去，小桥流水人家的景致再现峡谷。登仙桥以麻石砌筑，墩台嵌入岩石，长19米、宽6米、高6米，跨径17米。1912年，山洪暴发桥毁，1922年重建。为市级文物保护单位。

Dengxian Bridge

Dengxianqiao Village, Gugang Township, Le'an County, Jiangxi Province, built during 968-976 AD.

Since ancient times, Dengxian Bridge has served as a heavily contested battleground, and the bridge body has many scars from bullets. It is located in a long and narrow valley that is often wrapped by fog and has been the site of many well concealed ambushes. In 1933 AD, the First Front Army of the Chinese Workers' and Peasants' Red Army fought against the fourth "encirclement and suppression" in Dengxian Bridge. After several hours of fierce fighting, one division commander, one chief-of-staff, and one brigade commander were all taken captive. A batch of weapons and tens of thousands of silver coins were subsequently seized. This was known as "the victory of Huangpi". The valley, however, regained its tranquility after the war. The bridge is built with granite masonry, with its abutments embedded in the surrounding stone. The bridge is 19 meters long, 6 meters wide, 6 meters high, and has a span of 17 meters. The bridge was once destroyed in 1912 AD by a flash flood and was rebuilt in 1922 AD. Dengxian Bridge has been listed as a historical and cultural sites protected at the municipal level.

梅岭桥

江西省浮梁县瑶里镇梅岭村，宋代（960—1279年）

桥长9米、宽4米、高6米，为独孔石拱全砖石结构半阙型廊桥。廊桥连通的徽饶古道百余公里，山路皆由大块厚实花岗岩铺砌。桥两侧断断续续保留着几百米的古道遗存。徽饶古道已废弃，桥已无人行走。到瑶里古镇游览，可以到梅岭桥边春赏梅花、秋赏桂花。

Meiling Bridge

Meiling Village, Yaoli Town, Fuliang County, Jiangxi Province, built during 960-1279 AD.

This single arch stone arch bridge has a brick structure. It is 9 meters long, 4 meters wide, and 6 meters high. The bridge is located along the ancient Huirao Road, where more than 100 kilometers of mountain roads are paved by massive pieces of thick granite. The Meiling Bridge served as an important node, and the two ends of the bridge are still connected to several hundred meters of old road. The ancient Huirao Road has become overgrown, and Meiling Bridge is no longer crossed. Still, people will go to the bridge to enjoy plum blossoms in spring and fragrans in the autumn.

古莲桥

江苏省昆山市锦溪古镇，南宋（1127—1279 年）

据传，宋孝宗赵昚（1163—1189 年在位）与爱妃陈氏一同到锦溪品尝湖鲜，流连山水。陈妃不幸早逝，令宋孝宗难以释怀，就将她安葬在锦溪小湖岛，并钦赐建造庙宇、楼阁亭台、水榭画舫。古莲桥是莲池禅院的附属建筑。后古莲桥残损毁塌。1996 年，苏州市文物部门出资将陈妃水墓、莲池禅院、古莲桥一并复建。

Gulian Bridge

Jinxi Ancient Town, Kunshan, Jiangsu Province, built during 1127-1279 AD.

According to legend, Emperor Zhao Shen of the Song Dynasty (1163-1189 AD) and his beloved concubine Chen went to Jinxi to taste fresh delicacies and to linger among the mountains and waters. Concubine Chen's subsequent unfortunate and early death was hard on Zhao Shen. He buried her in a small lake island in Jinxi and built a temple, a pavilion-pagoda, and a pleasure boat structure there in her honor. Gulian Bridge is a component of the Lianchi Temple. Previously, the bridge was damaged and collapsed. In 1996, the cultural relics department of Suzhou invested in the reconstruction of Concubine Chen's water tomb, Lianchi Temple, and the Gulian Bridge.

广济桥

浙江省宁波市奉化区江口街道南渡村，北宋建隆二年（961 年）

又名南渡桥，北宋绍圣三年（1096 年）奉化主簿李肃主持募捐，百姓相助重建。南宋绍熙元年（1190 年）建成两墩三孔木石砖瓦结构廊桥，长 51.68 米，宽 6.6 米。元世祖至元二十三年（1286 年）主簿卢振龙主持复建，两侧加建石亭一座。明洪武（1368—1398 年）、天启（1621—1627 年），清雍正（1723—1735 年）、乾隆（1736—1795 年）、嘉庆（1796—1820 年）年间和 1986 年大修。为全国重点文物保护单位。

Guangji Bridge

Nandu Village, Jiangkou Sub-district, Fenghua District, Ningbo, Zhejiang Province, built in 961 AD.

Guangji Bridge, also known as Nandu Bridge, was rebuilt in 1096 AD when Li Su, the secretary of Fenghua County raised donations for it, together with additional assistance from local people. In 1190 AD, it was retrofitted as a timber stone and brick covered bridge with tiles. It contains two piers and three spans. It is 51.68 meters long, and 6.6 meters wide. In 1286 AD, the county secretary Lu Zhenlong oversaw the restoration of the bridge, and added a stone pavilion at each of its sides. The bridge underwent extensive repairs in the Hongwu(1368-1398 AD) and Tianqi(1621-1627 AD) periods of the Ming Dynasty, the Yongzheng(1723-1735 AD), Qianlong(1736-1795 AD) and Jiaqing(1796-1820 AD) periods of the Qing Dynasty, and also in 1986. It has been listed as a major historical and cultural sites protected at the national level.

百梁桥

浙江省宁波市海曙区洞桥镇鄞江，宋代（960—1279 年）

  该桥使用一百余根杉木架设横梁，故而得名，号称"浙东第一桥"。唐神龙元年（705 年）建起木船连板的"浮梁桥"。北宋熙宁元年（1068 年），邑首朱文伟筹谋建桥，惜未动工病逝。其子朱用谧继承父志捐资，百姓协助，于北宋元丰元年（1078 年）建成长约 100 米、宽 7 米、高 10 米的六墩七孔石墩木梁廊桥。后廊桥北端焚毁，朱老太公孙子朱世则、朱世弥重建。朱氏三代善举千年流芳。元顺帝（1333—1368 年），明成化（1465—1487 年），清嘉庆（1796—1820 年）、咸丰（1851—1861 年）、光绪（1875—1908 年）年间修缮。

Bailiang Bridge

over Yinjiang River, Dongqiao Town, Haishu District, Ningbo, Zhejiang Province, built during 960-1279 AD.

The lower part of the bridge's lookout structure uses over 100 horizontal beams made of China fir, and this is where its name comes from. It is known as the "Number One Bridge in East Zhejiang". It was built in 705 AD as a "floating beam bridge", a pontoon bridge consisting of connected timber boats. In 1068 AD, Zhu Wenwei, the head of the region, prepared plans for the construction of a bridge, but he died before the work started. His son Zhu Yongmi then carried out his father's wish by donating funds for a bridge, and was aided by the efforts of local people. As a result, in 1078 AD, they completed a covered bridge approximately 100 meters long, 7 meters wide, and 10 meters high. It has six piers and seven spans, and is composed of stone piers and timber beams. The northern part was later destroyed in a fire which was rebuilt by the grandsons of great-grandfather Zhu—Zhu Shize and Zhu Shimi. The kindness of Zhu's three generations has been passed down for a long time. Bailiang Bridge was restored in the Shundi (1333-1368 AD) period of the Yuan Dynasty, the Chenghua (1465-1487 AD) period of the Ming Dynasty, and the Jiaqing (1796-1820 AD), Xianfeng (1851-1861 AD) and Guangxu (1875-1908 AD) periods of the Qing Dynasty.

广济桥

广东省潮州市,南宋乾道七年(1171年)

该桥于南宋乾道七年(1171年)始建。长518米,石墩、石梁廊桥,有亭屋126间,西端十二墩长137.3米,东端八墩长283.4米,之间由18只小船托载浮桥连接。每日上午10时,浮桥连接百姓通行,下午5时,浮桥撤走船只航行。于清雍正二年(1724年)放置在西桥八墩、东桥十二墩上的两尊硕大铁牛,于清道光二十二年(1842年)被洪水冲走一尊。民谣传:"潮州湘桥好风流,十八梭船二十四洲,二十四楼台二十四样,二只牲牛一只溜。"广济桥与赵州桥、洛阳桥、卢沟桥并称中国古代四大名桥,同列全国重点文物保护单位。

Guangji Bridge

Chaozhou, Guangdong Province, built in 1171 AD.

Guangji Bridge was first built in 1171 AD. The bridge is 518 meters long and is supported by stone piers and stone beams. Its gallery house pavilion structure has 126 bays. It is composed of three parts; the west end has 12 piers and is 137.3 meters long; the east end has 8 piers and is 283.4 meters long; and its pontoon bridge in the middle is spanned by 18 small floating boats. At 10 o'clock in the morning, the pontoon bridge is linked with the other two segments, allowing people to travel along it. After 5 p.m. the middle section is opened, and only boats can pass. In 1724 AD, two huge ox statues made of iron were cast, one placed on the 8th pier of the west bridge segment, and the other on the 12th pier of the east bridge segment. In 1842 AD, however, one of the statues was lost to a flood. As a folksong describes, "The bridge scene is so great, 18 ships, 24 lands, 24 pavilions and 24 shapes, 2 farm cattles, and one that escapes!" The bridge is renowned as one of China's four famous ancient bridges, the other three being Zhaozhou Bridge, Luoyang Bridge, and Lugou Bridge. These four bridges have all been listed as the major historical and cultural sites protected at the national level.

洪济桥

山西省襄汾县汾城镇南关石坡下，金大定二十三年（1183年）

汾城镇古称太平县。洪济桥东西走向，明嘉靖（1522—1566年）、万历（1573—1620年）、天启（1621—1627年）、清康熙（1662—1722年）、乾隆（1736—1795年）年间修缮。洪济桥连通陕川两省重要驿道，西疙瘩城门楼尚存，是官道大路关口。1920年大水将桥冲毁，县长纪泽蒲倡导集资重修。

Hongji Bridge

down the stone slope of the south gate of Fencheng Town, Xiangfen County, Shanxi Province, built in 1183 AD.

Fencheng Town was historically known as Taiping County. The east-west bridge was renovated during the Jiajing (1522-1566 AD), Wanli (1573-1620 AD), and Tianqi (1621-1627 AD) periods of the Ming Dynasty and during the Kangxi (1662-1722 AD) and Qianlong (1736-1795 AD) periods of the Qing Dynasty. It connected the official courier route connecting Shaanxi and Sichuan. The west gate tower of the town—which served as the entry point for the ancient state highway—has been preserved. A flood in 1920 AD destroyed the bridge, after which county's magistrate Ji Zepu organized fundraising efforts to rebuild it.

中 国 廊 桥 精 粹
The Quintessence of Covered Bridges in China

元 代

1271—1368 年

　　元代建造的廊桥数量不多，但在传承的基础上有一定进步，起到承上启下作用。这一时期，在不同地区建造的廊桥均具有当地民居构造的典型特征。位于成都市南河的安顺廊桥使威尼斯人马可·波罗（1254—1324 年）发出"世界之人无有能想象其甚者"的感慨，并将之写入《马可·波罗游记》。中国作家魏明伦所作《廊桥赋》雕刻于安顺廊桥题壁之上，是为廊桥文化一大奇观。安徽遗存两座元代时期建造的廊桥，一座是呈坎村的环秀桥，一座是许村的高阳桥，规模不大但都是历史文化精品，受到当地乡民的精心保护和游人的喜爱。

Yuan Dynasty

(1271–1368 AD)

During the Yuan Dynasty, the number of covered bridges constructed was limited; however, there was some progress on the basis of inheritance, playing a role in connecting the past and the future. During this period, the covered bridges built in different regions all had the typical characteristics of local residential structures. The Anshun Covered Bridge, located on the Nanhe River in Chengdu, Sichuan Province, inspired the Venetian Marco Polo (1254-1324 AD) to exclaim that "no one in the world could imagine its grandeur", and he wrote about it in *The Travels of Marco Polo. The Ode to the Covered Bridge* written by Chinese writer Wei Minglun is carved on the wall of the Anshun Covered Bridge, which is a great wonder of the culture of covered bridges. There are two covered bridges built during the Yuan Dynasty in Anhui Province, one is Huanxiu Bridge in Chengkan Village, and the other is Gaoyang Bridge in Xucun Village. Although they are not large in scale, but are both historical and cultural treasures that have been carefully protected by local villagers and loved by tourists.

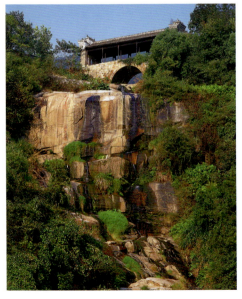

灵润桥

湖北省黄梅县大河镇四祖寺村四祖寺，元至正元年（1341年）

又名花桥、四祖寺桥。单孔敞廊式廊桥，石墩木柱、木梁木檩，单脊双坡顶覆小青瓦。长20米、宽6米、高5米、跨径7.4米。两端使用青砖建高大券顶式五花山门，门口石壁雕刻飞禽走兽。桥下岩石遗留古人石刻，据传，"碧玉流"三个大字是唐代书法家柳公权题写。为省级文物保护单位。

Lingrun Bridge

Sizu Temple, Sizusi Village, Dahe Town, Huangmei County, Hubei Province, built in 1341 AD.

Also known as Huaqiao Bridge or Sizusi Bridge. This is an arch covered bridge with timber beams, columns, purlins, and stone piers. It has a single span. Its roof has a single ridge and double slopes covered with small grey tiles. The bridge is 20 meters long, 6 meters wide, 5 meters high, and its span is 7.4 meters. Grey bricks are used at both ends to build tall and large multicolored gates with arched roofs. Flying birds and walking beasts are carved on the gate walls. A stone under the bridge is inscribed with the phrase "the Green Jade Flows". It is said that, these characters were inscribed by Liu Gongquan, a calligrapher of the Tang Dynasty. It has been listed as a historical and cultural sites protected at the provincial level.

半路亭桥

浙江省庆元县黄田镇陈边村，元至正（1341—1368年）

又名云岩桥、查洋桥。伸臂式木拱廊桥，东西走向，长28米、宽4.9米、高5.2米、跨径21.2米，九开间，双檐悬山顶，中设双层飞檐阁楼铺小青瓦，两侧安置三叠遮雨板。清嘉庆二十三年（1818年）、1917年整修。属于处州廊桥，为全国重点文物保护单位。

Banluting Bridge

Chenbian Village, Huangtian Town, Qingyuan County, Zhejiang Province, built during 1341-1368 AD.

Banluting Bridge, also known as Yunyan Bridge or Chayang Bridge, is a timber cantilever arch bridge that runs in east-west direction. It is 28 meters long, 4.9 meters wide, and 5.2 meters high, with a span of 21.2 meters. It has a gallery house with 9 bays. It is covered by a double-eave, overhanging gable roof with upturned eaves, and topped with small grey tiles. Three-layer awnings are installed at both side of the bridge to protect it from rain. The bridge was repaired in 1818 AD and 1917 AD. Banluting Bridge is classified as Chuzhou Covered Bridges, which have been listed as a major historical and cultural sites protected at the national level.

回龙桥

浙江省武义县郭洞村，元代（1271—1368 年）

古村因岭环如郭、幽深似洞而得名郭洞。世人有"郭外风光古，洞中日月长"的赞叹。回龙桥又名石虹桥，位于郭洞村水口要津。单孔石拱凉亭式廊桥，亭顶设龙脊飞檐，顶尖宝葫芦象征吉祥如意。明隆庆（1567—1572 年）年间、清康熙六十年（1721 年）整修。

Huilong Bridge

Guodong Village, Wuyi County, Zhejiang Province, built during 1271-1368 AD.

The village's name, Guodong derives from the high mountains that surround it like a high city wall (*guo*) and which are deep and cavernous like a cave (*dong*). Mortals have praised the village with the verse, "The scenery outside Guo is ancient, days and nights in Dong are long". Huilong Bridge, also known as Shihong Bridge, is located at the inlet and outlet of the river in Guodong Village. It is a stone arch cool-pavilion-style covered bridge with single span. The pavilion roof has a dragon-shaped ridge with upturned eaves. On its top is the figure of a precious gourd that symbolizes good luck. The bridge was repaired sometime during 1567-1572 AD as well as in 1721 AD.

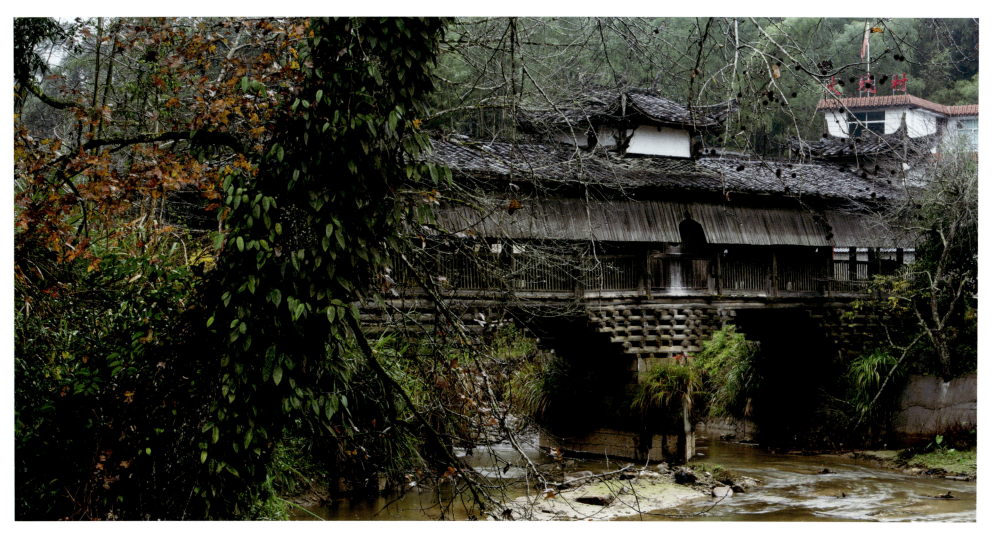

仁寿桥

福建省泰宁县下渠镇大坑村仁寿溪，元延祐元年（1314年）

明弘治元年（1488年）、清嘉庆十六年（1811年）、1969年大修。仁寿桥为客家传统建筑风格（坚固安全、封闭、融于自然），双桥堍、独墩两孔、全木结构廊桥，东西走向，长27米、宽4.65米、高7米，九开间，船首形石砌桥墩与两座桥堍上叠搭十层交叉（俗称"喜鹊窝"）伸臂圆木，将粗大平梁平稳托起，桥面夯土平实便于车马通过。单脊悬山顶满铺小青瓦，中间建飞檐翘角小阁楼，两端建对角翘檐牌坊。木质雨披内安置护栏、长条凳。

Renshou Bridge

Renshou Creek, Dakeng Village, Xiaqu Town, Taining County, Fujian Province, built in 1314 AD.

This bridge was overhauled in 1488 AD, 1811 AD, and 1969. Renshou Bridge is an example of traditional architecture of the Hakka Nationality (known for structural stability and safety, closed-forms, and integration with nature). It is a timber frame bridge with one pier and two spans. It runs from east to west and is 27 meters long, 4.65 meters wide, and 7 meters high. Its gallery house has 9 bays. The ship-bow shaped stone piers as well as structures on both ends of the bridge hold ten layers of intersecting cantilevered logs (referred to locally as a magpie nest) which steadily support the bridge's thick horizontal log beams. The bridge deck's tamped earth allows carts and horses to travel across smoothly. The bridge's single-ridge overhanging gable roof is covered by small grey tiles, and in the center, there is a small pavilion with upturned eaves and upturned corners. Both ends of the bridge are framed with memorial archways. Under the wooden awnings are guardrails and long benches.

环秀桥

安徽省黄山市徽州区呈坎镇呈坎村，元代（1271—1368 年）

始建于元代。环秀桥是溪东街和前后街的通道，并连接休宁县通往许村、歙县县城的要道。五孔石桥（现为两墩三孔），长 26.65 米、宽 3.85 米、高 4.55 米，廊屋占整桥的三分之一。为全国重点文物保护单位。2024 年 6 月，环秀桥受洪水强烈冲击，木结构桥亭被冲毁，石质桥面、桥墩暂时完好。

Huanxiu Bridge

Chengkan Village, Chengkan Town, Huizhou District, Huangshan, Anhui Province, built during 1271-1368 AD.

Huanxiu Bridge was originally constructed during 1271-1368 AD. Huanxiu Bridge serves as a passage between Xidong Street and Qianhou Street, and it also connects the main road from Xiuning County to Xucun Village and Shexian County. This five-arch stone bridge (currently with two piers and three arches) is 26.65 meters Long, 3.85 meters wide, and 4.55 meters high, with the covered corridor occupying one-third of the bridge's length. It has been listed as a major historical and cultural sites protected at the national level. In June 2024, HuanXiu Bridge was severely impacted by the flood. The wooden structure of the pavilion was washed away, while the stone bridge deck and piers remained intact for the time being.

高阳桥

安徽省歙县许村镇许村，元代（1271—1368 年）

诗人李白称赞许村"十里沙滩水中流，东西石壁秀而幽"，王安石、朱熹、文天祥、董其昌也留有诗文。高阳桥又名离合桥，乡绅许友山捐资募款建造。桥右侧是古渡口，左侧是明代石牌坊。为全国重点文物保护单位。

Gaoyang Bridge

Xucun Village, Xucun Town, Shexian County, Anhui Province, built during 1271-1368 AD.

Xucun Village was acclaimed by the renowned poet Li Bai, who stated it was a place where "ten *li* of beach the current flows between, the east and west rock walls are exquisite and faraway seen". Poems about the village were also penned by historically noted literati including Wang Anshi, Zhu Xi, Wen Tianxiang, and Dong Qichang. Also known as Lihe Bridge, the construction of the bridge was funded by a member of the local gentry, Xu Youshan. On the right side of the bridge locates an ancient ferry landing, and on the left stands a Ming Dynasty stone memorial archway. It has been listed as a major historical and cultural sites protected at the national level.

中 国 廊 桥 精 粹

The Quintessence of Covered Bridges in China

明 代

1368—1644 年

　　明代时期，廊桥建造师承前启后，在北起黄河岸边，南至云南、岭南的广大地域建设了众多名桥。这一时期，被誉为"无桥之桥"的木拱廊桥在浙江南部、福建北部以及更广阔的地区大量建造，跨径、长度及华美程度等都达到了历史高峰。同时，其他形制的廊桥也大量建造。廊桥内人性化设施更加完善，添置了木制长凳、床铺，有些地方在桥头兴建了店铺、客栈、茶室。廊桥从此成为除了寺庙、祠堂、戏台以外最为重要的公共设施和聚会场所。

Ming Dynasty

(1368–1644 AD)

During the Ming Dynasty, covered bridge builders built upon previous achievements and extended their reach from the banks of the Yellow River in the north to Yunnan and the Lingnan region in the south, constructing numerous notable bridges. In this period, the wooden arch covered bridge, often referred to as the "bridge without a bridge", was extensively constructed in southern Zhejiang, northern Fujian, and even broader areas, achieving historical peaks in span, length, and aesthetic sophistication. At the same time, many other types of covered bridges were constructed. These bridges were equipped with increasingly human-centered amenities, including wooden benches and beds. In some locations, shops, inns, and tea houses were established at the bridgeheads. As a result, covered bridges became the most important public facilities and gathering places, apart from temples, ancestral halls, and stages.

仙桥

山西省沁源县灵空山镇灵空山一线天绝壁，明代（1368—1644 年）

　　仙桥下有一块横亘在绝壁之间长约 3 米、宽 1 米的条石，即最早的"仙桥"。仙桥之险天下称奇，绝壁双峡仅隔尺余，下方峡谷深达数十米，越高越窄，几近弥合，自古人称"一线天"。单孔石拱，上建敞棚式廊屋三间，长 10 米、宽 3 米、高 9 米，双檐悬山顶红柱青瓦。仙桥连同圣寿寺主体建筑被列为全国重点文物保护单位。

Xianqiao Bridge

over the cliffs of a slot canyon at Lingkong Mountain in Lingkongshan Town, Qinyuan County, Shanxi Province, built during 1368-1644 AD.

The original Xianqiao Bridge was a stone slab measured 3 meters long and 1 meter wide, placed under the present structure. The current Xianqiao Bridge is located between precipitous cliffs of a canyon over a valley which is tens of meters deep. The Perilousness of the Xianqiao Bridge is renowned throughout the world. The width of the canyon narrows as its height increases. The tops of the cliffs of the two sides almost joined, and as a result it was referred to as the "single-line-sky" by ancient people. The present Xianqiao Bridge is a single-span stone arch covered bridge with 10 meters long, 3 meters wide and 9 meters high. Its three-bay gallery house is decorated with a double-eave overhanging gable roof covered by grey tiles and supported by red columns. The Xianqiao Bridge has been listed as a major historical and cultural sites protected at the national level together with the main body of the Shengshou Temple.

峦桥

山西省沁源县灵空山镇灵空山柏子河源头，明代中期

　　峦桥纵横叠木八层为梁，在长江以北独此一座。长17米、宽4米、高7米，丹柱画廊，门首、立柱上端及两柱之间安置彩绘圆雕"龙门雀替"（宋代《营造法式》称"绰幕"），悬山顶厚重朴素，顶脊两端有飞翘"鱼化龙"雕塑，造型优雅别致，装饰华丽美观。

Luanqiao Bridge

over the origin of Baizi River at Lingkong Mountain in Lingkongshan Town, Qinyuan County, Shanxi Province, built in the middle of the Ming Dynasty.

The Luanqiao Bridge has eight layers of criss-crossing beams and is the only one of its kind north of the Yangtze River. It is 17 meters long, 4 meters wide, and 7 meters high, and sports an overhanging gable roof. Its gallery house is decorated with paintings and is supported by red columns. Colored decorated *longmen queti* (dragon-gate sparrow braces, also known as *chuomu* in the Song Dynasty construction manual *Yingzao Fashi*) were carved and installed on the gateways as well as between and on top of the columns, creating a simple but solemn style. There are *dragon fish* (a fish that is in the process of becoming a dragon) sculptures at both ends of the roof ridge, the unique shape of which is beautiful and elegant.

环翠桥

山西省介休市洪山镇石屯村,明嘉靖十九年（1540年）

楼阁式的环翠桥因宛若天成,自古被赞为"小天宫"。石砌两墩三孔（河道断流）,24根木柱支撑三重檐歇山式四角宝顶,二层原为"望云台",后辟为玉皇阁,供奉玉皇大帝并四天神。各层顶部满铺绿黄釉琉璃瓦及其他琉璃构件,连接部榫卯衔扣稳固无摧,至今安过车马造福后人。据主跨顶端功德碑记,为刘氏族众刘子思、刘子葱、刘子恩、刘子慈等筹资倡建。

Huancui Bridge

Shitun Village, Hongshan Town, Jiexiu, Shanxi Province, built in 1540 AD.

The pavilion-style Huancui Bridge, praised since ancient times as a "Little Heavenly Palace" for its natural elegance, is constructed with two stone piers and three arches (the river channel is currently dry). Twenty-four wooden pillars support a three-tiered hip-and-gable roof with a four-cornered precious top. The second floor, originally named "*Wangyuntai*" (Cloud Viewing Platform), was later converted into the Jade Emperor Pavilion, dedicated to the Jade Emperor and the Four Heavenly Kings. The roofs of each tier are fully covered with green and yellow glazed tiles and other glazed components. The mortise and tenon joints connecting the parts are sturdy and undamaged, allowing the bridge to endure vehicular traffic and benefit generations. According to the merit stele at the top of the main span, the bridge was funded and initiated by members of the Liu family, including Liu Zisi, Liu Zicong, Liu Zien, and Liu Zici.

断涧仙桥

甘肃省漳县贵清山，明隆庆元年（1567年）

断涧仙桥跨越海拔2340米的中、西峰之间，是中国地势最险要的廊桥。顶峰遗存明隆庆（1567—1572年）年间建造的中峰寺，断涧仙桥、小山门桥是香客上香的唯一通道。有记载的大修、重建共十八次，前十七次维持木平梁硬山顶廊桥形制，长13.6米、宽1.8米、自高2.6米，距悬崖谷底600余米。2013年，断涧仙桥因腐朽垮落深谷，2014年重建。

Duanjian Xianqiao Bridge

Guiqing Mountain, Zhangxian County, Gansu Province, built in 1567 AD.

Duanjian Xianqiao Bridge spans the mountain's middle and west peaks, which rise 2,340 meters above sea level, and it is the most steep and dangerous covered bridge. The Duanjian Xianqiao Bridge and Xiaoshanmen Bridge are the only channels through which pilgrims can use to travel to Zhongfeng Temple built during 1567-1572 AD. According to records, this bridge was renovated or rebuilt 18 times, the first 17 times of which it maintained its timber beam covered bridge structure with a flush gable roof over its gallery house. This bridge is 13.6 meters long, 1.8 meters wide, 2.6 meters high, and rises more than 600 meters above the valley below. In 2013, Duanjian Xianqiao Bridge collapsed due to rot and was rebuilt in 2014.

灞陵桥

甘肃省渭源县城渭水河,明代(1368—1644年)

初为木平梁桥,清同治末年甘肃提督梅开泰重建。1919年,县长黎之彦主持,乡绅白玉端、徐立朝出资督理,陇西木工名师莫如珍掌尺,建成纯木结构单梁悬臂廊桥。1934年改为叠梁木拱廊桥。西北走向,长40米、宽4.8米、高16米、跨径30米、十三开间,是西北地区唯一大型木拱廊桥。为全国重点文物保护单位。

Baling Bridge

Weishui River, Weiyuan county, Gansu Province, built during 1368-1644 AD.

Originally, Baling Bridge was a timber beam bridge, and later it was rebuilt under the supervision of Mei Kaitai, provincial commander-in-chief of Gansu Province at the last years of the Tongzhi period of the Qing Dynasty. In 1919 AD, under the direction of county magistrate Li Zhiyan, funded by local gentry Bai Yuduan and Xu Lichao, and through the work of famous carpenter Mo Ruzhen, the bridge was rebuilt as a single-beam timer cantilever covered bridge. In 1934 AD, the bridge was reconstructed as a single-span timber combined beam-arch bridge (also referred to as a redundant beam-arch bridge). It has a gallery house with 13 bays and is 40 meters long, 4.8 meters wide, and 16 meters tall. It has a net span of 30 meters. It is the only large timber arch covered bridge in northwest China, it has been listed as a major historical and cultural sites protected at the national level.

龙凤桥

甘肃省康县平洛镇团庄村，明洪武二年（1369年）

陇南市文物部门于2009年在康县望关乡发现半块古石碑（存康县博物馆），只有44个阴刻楷体字可辨。其中，"茶马贩通番捷路"证实陇南"北茶马古道"存在。龙凤桥为叠木平梁全木结构廊桥，长16米、宽3.6米、高3.6米，七开间，连接北茶马古道的"平乐古道"段。圆木纵横排列，逐层叠伸，支撑粗长木梁组成基础架构。穿斗式廊屋，檩脚遗留四象、四龙、两凤木雕。为省级文物保护单位。

Longfeng Bridge

Tuanzhuang Village, Pingluo Town, Kangxian County, Gansu Province, built in 1369 AD.

In 2009, the Longnan Cultural Relics Department found half of an ancient stone tablet (now part of the collection of the Kangxian Museum) in Wangguan Township, Kangxian County. On this tablet, only forty-four incised carving regular script characters can be recognized, but among them is a phrase referring to horse and tea vendors to border areas, proving the existence of a northern Ancient Tea Horse Road in southern Gansu. The Longfeng Bridge is part of the Pingle segment of this road. It is a combined-beam timber covered bridge. It is 16 meters long, 3.6 meters wide, 3.6 meters high, and has a gallery house on top with 7 bays. Logs on the bridge overlap in a criss-crossing manner, and thick and long supporting timbers form a foundational structure. The gallery house is a *chuandou* style structure, and there are wood carvings of four elephants, four dragons, and two phoenixes on the purlin ends. It has been listed as a historical and cultural sites protected at the provincial level.

云龙桥

甘肃省榆中县兴隆山，明代（1368—1644年）

明末被洪水冲毁，清乾隆（1736—1795年）年间知县唐鸣钟重建，取名唐公桥。清嘉庆（1796—1820年）年间再次重建。清光绪二十六年（1900年），甘肃省布政使岑春煊拨一千两白银复建后，更名云龙桥。这座桥的底部现已替换为加固混凝土拱（梁）。桥长15米、宽3米，七开间，桥的两头各有一阁，是歇山顶四角飞檐的建筑。廊内雕梁画栋，廊顶覆盖琉璃瓦。为省级文物保护单位。

Yunlong Bridge

Xinglong Mountain, Yuzhong County, Gansu Province, built during 1368-1644 AD.

The bridge was destroyed by floods in the late Ming Dynasty. During 1736-1795 AD, Tang Mingzhong, the county magistrate, ordered craftsmen to rebuild it and renamed it Tanggong Bridge. The bridge was later reconstructed during 1796-1820 AD. In 1900 AD, Cen Chunxuan, the governor of Gansu Province, allotted 1,000 taels of silver to rebuild the bridge and renamed it as Yunlong Bridge. The lower part of the bridge was then replaced by a reinforced concrete arch. The bridge is 15 meters long and 3 meters wide. There are 7 bays on the gallery house, and each end of the bridge has a pavilion with a hip and gable roof, overhanging eaves, and cornice. The gallery house's internal columns are covered with painted decorations, and the roof top is covered by glazed tiles. The bridge has been listed as a historical and cultural sites protected at the provincial level.

映月桥

四川省松潘县松潘古城，明永乐（1403—1424年）

松潘古称松州，初设于汉代。映月桥有"岷江上游第一桥"之誉。明永乐年间，由官府倡导、大商户出资、百姓出力，在城西南修建一座木平梁殿阁式廊桥，跨越岷江，将古城各村落与松潘草地连接起来。据传，桥旁岩顶大悲寺佛头上曾有一颗夜明珠，映照桥下水面，犹如一轮明月，故称映月桥。

Yingyue Bridge

Songpan Old Town, Songpan County, Sichuan Province, built during 1403-1424 AD.

Songpan, known as Songzhou in ancient times, was first set in the Han Dynasty. Yingyue Bridge was honored as the "first bridge in the upper reaches of the Minjiang River". During 1403-1424 AD, the government advocated that a bridge be built in the area. Rich merchants invested in the project, and common people contributed to its construction. In the southwest of the city, a timber beam palace and pavilion covered bridge was built, crossing the Minjiang River, and connecting the ancient city's villages with the Songpan grassland. It is said that a legendary luminous pearl on the head of the Buddha of Dabei Temple (located on a rock outcropping beside the bridge) casts light on the surface of the water under the bridge, just like a bright moon. As a result, the bridge is called "Yingyue Bridge".

太极桥

云南省腾冲市腾越街道大盈江瀑布顶峰,明代(1368—1644年)

清光绪七年(1881年)重修。为石墩石梁、石阶石柱、石栏石雀替、石斗拱石橼、石扁石顶筑成的亭式廊桥,南北对称,两孔跨径各5.5米,船首形桥墩牢踞河心岩石墩,高1.7米,两端叠梁悬臂支撑桥亭,连接两岸。石亭高4.8米、宽3.5米,桥墩东西两侧有龟首蛇尾石雕。精妙独特,秀丽至美,坚固耐久。为市级文物保护单位。

Taiji Bridge

the peak of the Dayingjiang Waterfall, Tengyue Sub-district, Tengchong, Yunnan Province, built during 1368-1644 AD.

It was rebuilt in 1881 AD. This pavilion style covered bridge is composed of piers, beams, steps, columns, railings, sparrow braces (*queti*), *dougong* brackets, plaques, and a roof, all made of stone. Its symmetrical pair of north-south spans each cover a distance of 5.5 meters. The ship-bow shaped pier on the rock in the river's center is 1.7 meters tall. The two ends of the combined beam cantilevers supporting the bridge pavilion are attached to each of the respective banks. The stone pavilion is 4.8 meters high and 3.5 meters wide. On the east and west sides of the pier, there are stone carving with tortoise heads and snake tails. Exquisite, unique, elegant, strong, and unbroken, it is a renowned masterpiece. It has been listed as a historical and cultural sites protected at the municipal level.

刘家桥

湖北省咸宁市咸安区桂花镇刘家桥村，明代（1368—1644年）

为营造"小桥流水人家"的意境，刘氏先民在池塘水口建造了一座朴素雅致的廊桥。傍晚时，老人在廊桥相聚，常有"不求富贵命，但愿子孙贤"的谈论，路人多为老人们爽朗的笑声所感染。单孔石拱廊桥，长20米、宽5米、高6米、跨径10米。桥廊顶梁雕龙凤、八卦图案，两端建牌坊式门厅，双坡顶覆小青瓦。桥侧2米高青砖方孔花格护墙，下设长凳。

Liujia Bridge

Liujiaqiao Village, Guihua Town, Xian'an District, Xianning, Hubei Province, built during 1368-1644 AD.

In order to manifest the Chinese artistic and poetic trope of "family houses hidden past a narrow bridge under which a quiet creek flows", the ancestors of the Liu lineage built a simple and elegant covered bridge over the inlet that flows into their village pond. In the evenings, the elders of the village often gather there and can often be heard talking of "not desiring wealth, but wishing their children and grandchildren live virtuous lives". The laughter and nice words from such conversations are infectious to people passing by. The stone arch bridge is 20 meters long, 5 meters wide, 6 meters high, and has a span of 10 meters. A dragon, a phoenix, and the Eight Diagrams are carved into the top beam of the bridge's gallery house. Both ends of the structure have entrances built in the style of a memorial archway with a double-sloped roof covered with small grey tiles. Both sides of the bridge have a 2-meter-high grey brick lattice protective wall, and beside the wall are long benches.

广济桥

湖南省宜章县笆篱镇车田村大刘家村玉水河，明代（1368—1644年）

明代始建，清道光七年（1827年）重建。一墩两孔，叠木伸臂式砖石与木构混合形制廊桥，长30.6米、宽4.2米、高8.5米，桥墩上面方形碉楼宽9米。为省级文物保护单位。"真意焚香何须面朝南海，诚心拜佛此处就是西天。"该桥桥联闻名四方。

Guangji Bridge

Yushui River, Daliujia Village, Chetian Village, Bali Town, Yizhang County, Hunan Province, built during 1368-1644 AD.

This bridge was originally built during 1368-1644 AD, and rebuilt in 1827 AD. The bridge has one pier and two spans. It is a timber cantilever covered bridge with a mixed stone and timber structure. Its cantilever assemblage is composed of combined timbers. It is 30.6 meters long, 4.2 meters wide, and 8.5 meters high. The square-shaped tower above the pier is 9 meters wide. The bridge has been listed as a historical and cultural sites protected at the provincial level. This bridge is decorated with a famous poem: "If incense is burned for a true motive, why must the southern seas be the direction faced? By sincerely worshipping Buddha, the Western Paradise is this very place."

虹桥

湖南省凤凰县沱江镇，明代（1368—1644年）

新西兰作家路易·艾黎把对凤凰城的感受归纳为"中国最美的小城"。虹桥为百姓提供晴雨两便、四季皆宜的通行便利，是凤凰城的标志。虹桥原名卧虹桥，长80米、宽8米、高12.3米，为两墩三孔石拱楼殿式廊桥，每孔跨径11.8米。廊桥上部共三层，底层供行人过江，中层设茶楼店铺，上层为望远楼。

Hongqiao Bridge

Tuojiang Town, Fenghuang County, Hunan Province, built during 1368-1644 AD.

New Zealand writer Rewi Alley summed up his feelings about Fenghuang by calling it "the most beautiful town in China". The Hongqiao Bridge is its most famed symbol. The bridge provides the common people of the town convenient transportation across the Tuojiang River in both rain and shine and in all four seasons. It was formerly known as the Wohong Bridge and is an arch-palace style covered bridge. The bridge is 80 meters long, 8 meters wide, and 12.3 meters high. It has two piers and three spans, which have spans of 11.8 meters. The bridge has three levels. The bottom floor is for pedestrian crossing, the middle floor is for tea houses or shops, and the upper one is an observation tower.

余庆桥

湖南省新化县高田村,明代（1368—1644年）

清水河余庆桥旁侧只有一户人家。户主老王奉养年老的父亲,携妻子、儿孙居住桥西。"一水、一桥、一人家"使人印象深刻。古称横板桥,长38米、宽4.5米、高6米,纵横叠木平梁、独孔全木结构。桥西端遗存清咸丰（1851—1861年）、清光绪（1875—1908年）与中华民国时期功德碑数方。其中,清道光《奉宪示禁碑》记："从来规约不监则弊灾多生,贼盗不除则良善难靖,因故立此禁碑,永禁来往差役乘轿。"

Yuqing Bridge

Gaotian Village, Xinhua County, Hunan Province, built during 1368-1644 AD.

There is only one family who lives by the bridge. Mr Wang lives to its west together with his elderly father, wife, children, and grandchildren. The phrase "one river, one bridge, one family" comes to mind. Such a scene is impressive. In the past, the bridge was known as Hengban Bridge. Spanning the Qingshui River, it has a single span. The deck's main supporting beams are arranged in a criss-cross pattern. It is 38 meters long, 4.5 meters wide and 6 meters high. At the west end of the bridge, there are several surviving steles dating from the Xianfeng (1851-1861 AD) period and Guangxu (1851-1908 AD) period of the Qing Dynasty and sometime during 1912-1949 AD. Among them, the *Fengxian Warning Stele* records that "Without enforcement of rules, harm and misfortune will often occur. Without eradicating thieves and robbers, it will be difficult to spread goodness. Thus, this warning stele is placed here, to permanently ban the use of sedan chairs by officials(*chaiyi*) traveling on duty." (i.e. servants of imperial officials riding in sedan chairs would be a sign of corruption)

龙津桥

湖南省芷江侗族自治县潕水河，明万历（1573—1620年）

明万历（1573—1620年）年间，宽云和尚募集白银一万五千两、粮食一万余石，建成十三墩十四孔、五层楼、七座塔，长246.7米、宽12.2米的巨型廊桥。抗日战争时期，为通过载重货车，撤除了桥廊、塔楼。冒着日军飞机的轮番轰炸，龙津桥承载抵抗的车轮滚滚向前。1945年8月21日16时，中国战区"受降仪式"在芷江七里村举行。龙津桥与亿万中国人民一起，见证了这一历史时刻，"天下第一功勋桥"名扬天下。1999年，龙津桥修复。

Longjin Bridge

Wushui River, Zhijiang Dong Autonomous County, Hunan Province, built during 1573-1620 AD.

During 1573-1620 AD, the monk Kuanyun raised 15,000 taels of silver and more than 10,000 *dan* (one *dan* is equivalent to about 100 liters) grains to build this large-scale covered bridge. It had a gallery house with five stories, resting on top of thirteen piers with fourteen spans. It was built together with seven pagodas. It is 246.7 meters long and 12.2 meters wide. During the War of Resistance Against Japan (1931-1945 AD), the gallery house and pagodas were removed to facilitate the movement of heavy trucks along the bridge. The bridge braved multiple bombing raids by Japanese aircraft as the wheels of resistance advanced forward. On August 21, 1945 AD, at 4 p.m., the surrender ceremony was held in Qili Village. Together with hundreds of millions of Chinese people, Longjin Bridge witnessed the historic moment. The "world's most meritorious bridge" was hence well-known throughout the world. In 1999, the bridge was restored.

万寿桥

湖南省溆浦县黄茅园镇龙潭河，明崇祯九年（1636年）

又名画桥。重檐阁楼式廊桥，东西走向，长60米、宽4米、高11米，二十四开间，四墩五孔。石砌桥墩、贯木叠拱、圆木平梁、木廊瓦顶。廊顶中部建造高4米的重檐六角攒尖顶塔阁。廊桥两端门厅建龙脊门枋，枋檐为四层如意斗拱式样。清乾隆八年（1743年）至1945年，有七次大的修缮。2013年被列为县级文物保护单位。

Wanshou Bridge

Longtan River, Huangmaoyuan Town, Xupu County, Hunan Province, built in 1636 AD.

Also known as Huaqiao Bridge. The bridge runs from east to west and has four piers and five spans. It is 60 meters long, 4 meters wide, and 11 meters high. Its gallery house has 24 bays and is built in the style of a pavilion building with a double-eave. The bridge's piers are made of stone work. Timbers are interconnected and piled to form the arch, and logs serve as the bridge deck's main supporting beams. The gallery house is topped with tiles. The middle of the gallery house has a 4-meter tall pagoda building installed on top, with a six-corner multiple-eave pyramidal roof. Both ends of the bridge have memorial arch gateways with dragon-shaped ridges, and eaves made with four layers of *ruyi dougong* brackets. The bridge underwent extensive restoration work seven times between 1743 AD and 1945 AD. In 2013, the bridge has been listed as a historical and cultural sites protected at the county level.

人和桥

广西壮族自治区三江侗族自治县良口乡和里村，明嘉靖（1522—1566年）

人和桥是三王宫（建于明嘉靖年间）的附属建筑，长49米、宽4.35米、高7.2米，1917年维修。为县级文物保护单位。

Renhe Bridge

Heli Village, Liangkou Township, Sanjiang Dong Autonomous County, Guangxi Zhuang Autonomous Region, built during 1522-1566 AD.

Renhe Bridge is an ancillary structure of the Sanwang Palace (constructed during 1522-1566 AD). It is 49 meters long, 4.35 meters wide, and 7.2 meters high, and it underwent repairs in 1917. It has been listed as a historical and cultural sites protected at the county level.

迴澜桥

广西壮族自治区富川瑶族自治县朝东镇油沐村，明万历（1573—1620年）

明崇祯十四年（1641年）、清道光十九年（1839年）重修，1987年维修。三孔石拱、桥亭阁楼组合式廊桥，全长37.54米，桥廊长30.43米、宽4.64米，每拱跨径各6.22米。迴澜桥与青龙桥毗邻，被当地百姓称为鸳鸯风雨桥。属于富川瑶族风雨桥群，为全国重点文物保护单位。

Huilan Bridge

Youmu Village, Chaodong Town, Fuchuan Yao Autonomous County, Guangxi Zhuang Autonomous Region, built during 1573-1620 AD.

The bridge was rebuilt in 1641 AD and 1839 AD, and repaired in 1987. It is a stone arch covered bridge with three spans. It is a combined covered bridge and pavilion structure. It is 37.54 meters long in total, and the bridge corridor is 27.5 meters long and 4.9 meters wide. Each of its spans is 6.22 meters. Huilan Bridge is adjacent to the Qinglong Bridge. Local people refer to the two as the yuanyang wind and rain bridges (*yuanyang* being a symbol in China of a loving couple). Huilan Bridge is classified as Fuchuan Yao Ethnicity Wind and Rain Bridges Cluster, which has been listed as a major historical and cultural sites protected at the national level.

青龙桥

广西壮族自治区富川瑶族自治县朝东镇油沐村，明天启（1621—1627 年）

单孔砖石结构阁楼式廊桥。全长 35.1 米，桥阁宽 7.6 米，桥廊长 27.5 米、宽 4.9 米。中部顶端建歇山顶飞檐小阁，北端耸立一座三层阁楼。东、南、北三面有门。清道光（1821—1850 年）年间《创修青龙亭题名记碑》载："其中以惟亭一座，路衢三通，创自有明。宅西宛若龙山之吐秀，故题其额曰青龙也。"属于富川瑶族风雨桥群，为全国重点文物保护单位。

Qinglong Bridge

Youmu Village, Chaodong Town, Fuchuan Yao Autonomous County, Guangxi Zhuang Autonomous Region, built during 1621-1627 AD.

This is a stone arch bridge with a single span. It is 35.1 meters long in total, the pavilion is 7.6 meters wide, and the bridge corridor is 27.5 meters long and 4.9 meters wide. Its center has a small pavilion with a hip and gable roof with upturned eaves. In its northern part, there is a three-story pavilion. There are gates to the east, south, and north. A stele from the Qing Dynasty's Daoguang period (1821-1850 AD) is titled *Memorial Stele for the Creation of the Qinglong and its Naming*, states, "In the middle sits a lone pavilion that became well known because of the three roads there. The west house is just as beautiful as the Longshan Mountain, so it is titled Qinglong." Qinglong Bridge is classified as Fuchuan Yao Ethnicity Wind and Rain Bridges Cluster, which has been listed as a major historical and cultural sites protected at the national level.

普济桥

浙江省松阳县玉岩镇玉岩村玉溪，明正德（1506—1521 年）

两孔石墩双向伸臂木梁廊屋桥，桥长 26.5 米、宽 5.5 米，东西两端桥台用条石错缝砌筑，中间桥墩用条石砌成分水雁翅，以减轻洪水对桥墩的冲击力，增强桥墩牢固度。墩台上纵横叠交五层垫木，即横向三层垫木，纵向两层伸臂梁。桥面木板铺设，上覆廊屋七间。属于处州廊桥，为全国重点文物保护单位。

Puji Bridge

Yuxi Creek, Yuyan Village, Yuyan Town, Songyang County, Zhejiang Province, built during 1506-1521 AD.

It is a bi-directional timber cantilever arch bridge, with two stone piers. The bridge is 26.5 meters long, 5.5 meters wide. The bridge abutments at both the east and west ends are constructed with staggered stone slabs, while the central pier is built with stone to form a water-dividing goose wing, designed to reduce the impact of floodwaters on the pier and enhance its stability. On top of the piers, five layers of wooden pads are arranged in a cross pattern, consisting of three layers of transverse pads and two layers of longitudinal cantilever beams. The bridge deck is covered with wooden planks, supporting a corridor with 7 bays. Puji Bridge is classified as Chuzhou Covered Bridges, which have been listed as a major historical and cultural sites protected at the national level.

佛殿桥

浙江省遂昌县龙洋乡黄赤村，明代（1368—1644年）

佛殿桥又名宝善桥，平梁式廊桥，长17.75米、宽4.8米。廊屋作为寺庙，排列大小佛龛，供奉观世音菩萨等十余尊神佛，正中悬挂"有求必应"帐幔。

Fodian Bridge

Huangchi Village, Longyang Township, Suichang County, Zhejiang Province, built during 1368-1644 AD.

Fodian Bridge, also known as Baoshan Bridge, is a flat-beam covered bridge. It is 17.75 meters long and 4.8 meters wide. The corridor functions as a temple, housing numerous Buddhist niches, including Guanyin and others. A hanging curtain inscribed with "You Qiu Bi Ying" (All requests will be answered) is displayed in the center.

宏济桥

浙江省遂昌县王村口镇，明代（1368—1644年）

初名济川石桥，是王村口镇桥东村、桥西村近万人相互交往的唯一通道。跨乌溪江，连通衢州至闽北、赣东古驿道。圆木交叉支撑平梁廊桥，长35米、宽5.4米、高9米，九开间，桥堡两栋双檐翘角，单脊悬山顶覆小青瓦。清光绪初年改名宏济桥。清代（1644—1911年）和1912—1949年间重建。1935年，中国工农红军挺进师师长粟裕曾在宏济桥上作"北上抗日"讲演。

Hongji Bridge

Wangcunkou Town, Suichang County, Zhejiang Province, built during 1368-1644 AD.

The original name of the bridge is Jichuan Shiqiao Bridge, it was the only way for almost ten thousand villagers of Qiaodong Village and Qiaoxi Village in Wangcunkou Town to travel back and forth and communicate. Crossing the Wuxi River, it formed a part of the ancient courier road that connected Quzhou to northern Fujian and eastern Jiangxi. Logs are interspersed to support the bridge's supporting beams. The covered bridge is 35 meters long, 5.4 meters wide, and 9 meters high. Its gallery house has 9 bays and is covered with an overhanging gable roof with a single ridge topped with small grey tiles. The bridge includes two structures bearing roofs with double-eaves and upturned corners. In the early part of the Guangxu period of the Qing Dynasty, the bridge was renamed to Hongji Bridge. The bridge was rebuilt during 1644-1911 AD and 1912-1949 AD. In 1935 AD, on the Hongji Bridge, Su Yu, division commander of the Chinese Workers' and Peasants' Red Army Advancement Division, made his speech on "going north to resist Japan".

毓秀桥

浙江省青田县阜山乡陈宅村,明万历四年(1576年)

单孔石拱砖石结构廊桥,依山跨溪,古树环绕,小巧秀丽,恬静质朴,很受村民喜爱。桥北镌有"毓秀桥"和"万历四年建造"的题记。数百年来几度修缮复建。长11.76米、宽3.3米、高3米、跨径4.7米,廊屋五间,外侧设立12根方形砖柱,中央两侧设廊栅靠背椅,四角攒尖阁楼覆小青瓦。桥面鹅卵石铺道。属于处州廊桥,为全国重点文物保护单位。

Yuxiu Bridge

Chenzhai Village, Fushan Township, Qingtian County, Zhejiang Province, built in 1576 AD.

Surrounded by ancient trees, this single-span stone arch covered bridge has a brick structure, and is situated beside mountains and rivers. It is much beloved by villagers because of its delicate, graceful, beautiful, and refined look. There are inscriptions of "Yuxiu Bridge" and "built in the fourth year of the Wanli reign (1576 AD)" at the north part of the bridge. It has been overhauled several times over the past several hundred years. The bridge is 11.76 meters long, 3.3 meters wide, 3 meters high, and has an arch that spans 4.7 meters. Its gallery house has 5 bays. There are 12 rectangular brick columns on the outer side of the gallery house, and in its center are chairs with backrests. The bridge has a pavilion with a four-corner pyramidal roof covered by small grey tiles. The bridge deck is covered with cobblestones. Yuxiu Bridge is classified as Chuzhou Covered Bridges, which have been listed as a major historical and cultural sites protected at the national level.

古溪桥

浙江省龙泉市小梅镇黄南村,明代(1368—1644年)

清道光十八年(1838年)重建,单孔石拱木廊桥,东西走向,跨古溪。桥全长51.75米、宽5.8米,九开间。两侧设置栏杆、长条凳,中间楼阁藻井下设神龛。重檐悬山顶两端建牌楼,多组老年木雕生动传神,具有较高艺术价值。属于处州廊桥,为全国重点文物保护单位。

Guxi Bridge

Huangnan Village, Xiaomei Town, Longquan, Zhejiang Province, built during 1368-1644 AD.

In 1838 AD, the bridge was rebuilt. This single-span stone arch timber covered bridge runs in an east-west direction, acrossing the Guxi Creek. It is 51.75 meters long in total, 5.8 meters wide, and has a gallery house with 9 bays. There are railings and benches on both sides; in the middle pavilion, there are shrines. Memorial archways are built at both ends of the overhanging gable roofs with multiple-eaves, and many old wood carvings here have a high artistic value. Guxi Bridge is classified as Chuzhou Covered Bridges, which have been listed as a major historical and cultural sites protected at the national level.

永和桥

浙江省龙泉市安仁镇，明成化元年（1465 年）

丽水（古称处州）一市八县木拱廊桥群号称"处州九龙"，永和桥最长称"龙首"，原名永宁桥。《龙泉县志》记："长 125.7 米、宽 7.5 米，桥下用条石筑桥墩，桥墩上用巨松纵横相叠，层层挑出形成桥跨，上覆硬木板。桥屋四十二间，中有桥阁。"三墩四孔全木结构廊桥高 13 米，两端建飞檐斗拱门楼。清顺治（1644—1661 年）年间焚毁，清康熙五十七年（1718 年）重建，改名永安桥。清咸丰五年（1855 年），洪水冲塌两墩，复修改名永和桥。现存为 1914 年修建。属于处州廊桥，为全国重点文物保护单位。

Yonghe Bridge

Anren Town, Longquan, Zhejiang Province, built in 1465 AD.

The timber arch covered bridges in the eight counties under the prefectural jurisdiction of Lishui (which was formerly known as Chuzhou) are called "The Nine Dragons of Chuzhou". Yonghe Bridge is the longest among them and hence is called "the Dragon Head". Its original name was Yongning Bridge. It states in the *Longquan County Chronicle* that, "The bridge is 125.7 meters long, 7.5 meters wide. The bridge's piers are composed of strips of stones. On the piers, giant pines overlap vertically and horizontally, rising layer by layer to support the hardwood boards that cover the bridge span. The gallery house has 42 bays, and includes a pavilion in its center." It has three piers and four spans. Its gate buildings are on either side with *dougong* brackets and upturned eaves. Sometime during 1644-1661 AD, it burned down. And then it was rebuilt in 1718 AD and renamed Yongan Bridge. In 1855 AD, two piers were destroyed by floods, and its name was changed once again to the Yonghe Bridge upon being restored. The existing covered bridge was built in 1914 AD. Yonghe Bridge is classified as Chuzhou Covered Bridges, which have been listed as a major historical and cultural sites protected at the national level.

兰溪桥

浙江省庆元县五大堡乡西洋村松源溪,明万历二年(1574年)

原址位于兰溪村,谢子隆、吴丰募资建造。清乾隆四十八年(1783年)水毁,清乾隆五十九年(1794年)吴星海募资重建。因兰溪桥处在新修水库蓄水区,政府拨款 5.15 万元,桐梓村捐杉木 19 立方米,黄皮村捐杉木 18 立方米,桥阳村捐杉木 15 立方米,1984 年将兰溪桥整体搬迁至现址。伸臂式木拱廊桥,长 48.12 米、宽 5 米、高 9.8 米、跨径 36.8 米,十九开间。属于处州廊桥,为全国重点文物保护单位。

Lanxi Bridge

Songyuan Creek, Xiyang Village, Wudabao Township, Qingyuan County, Zhejiang Province, built in 1574 AD.

Lanxi Bridge formerly located in Lanxi Village, was built with initial funds raised by Xie Zilong and Wu Feng. In 1783 AD, the bridge was destroyed by flood, and in 1794 AD, Wu Xinghai raised funds for its restoration. In 1984, the bridge was relocated to its present site because its former location was to be covered by a new reservoir. The government allotted 51,500 yuan for the relocation and rebuilding. In addition, Tongzi Village donated 19 fir trees, Huangpi Village donated 18 fir trees, and Qiaoyang Village donated 15 fir trees for the project. It is a timber cantilever arch covered bridge, 48.12 meters long, 5 meters wide, 9.8 meters high, and has a span of 36.8 meters. Its gallery house has 19 bays. Lanxi Bridge is classified as Chuzhou Covered Bridges, which have been listed as a major historical and cultural sites protected at the national level.

如龙桥

浙江省庆元县举水乡月山村,明天启五年(1625年)

现桥为明天启五年重建。宋元王朝更替,"延陵望族,三让世家"的吴氏一支迁至月山村后,修祠堂、建庙宇、竖佛塔,同时建造了"二里十桥的廊桥峡谷"。如龙桥长28.2米、宽5.09米、跨径19.5米,九开间,圆木支撑拱架与全木结构廊屋组合。桥楼北高南低似龙的首尾,古称"蜈蚣桥"。属于处州廊桥,为全国重点文物保护单位。

Rulong Bridge

Yueshan Village, Jushui Township, Qingyuan County, Zhejiang Province, built in 1625 AD.

The existing bridge was rebuilt in 1625 AD. The bridge is located in "Covered Bridges Valley", and built by the Wu family, which was an influential lineage from the time spanning the Song to the Yuan dynasties. They built shrines, temples, and pagodas after moving to Yueshan Village. They also organized the building of the "Two *Li* Ten Covered Bridges Valley". Rulong Bridge is 28.2 meters long, 5.09 meters wide, and has a span of 19.5 meters, and has a gallery house with 9 bays. It is a woven timber arch-beam bridge. The bridge's northern structures are higher than those in the south, resembling the head and tail of a dragon. In the past, it was called Wugong Bridge. Rulong Bridge is classified as Chuzhou Covered Bridges, which have been listed as a major historical and cultural sites protected at the national level.

明代 1368—1644年

白云桥

浙江省庆元县举水乡月山村，明代（1368—1644 年）

始建于明代。白云桥位于月山村半山腰，是月山村五座廊桥中位置最高的。桥下飞瀑直泻状若白云，故得此名。叠梁木拱廊桥，南北走向，长 8 米、宽 3 米、跨径 7.5 米，双飞檐歇山顶满覆小青瓦。

Baiyun Bridge

Yueshan Village, Jushui Township, Qingyuan County, Zhejiang Province, built during 1368-1644 AD.

Baiyun Bridge, was originally constructed during 1368-1644 AD. The bridge was built in the middle of the mountain in Yueshan Village. As the highest among the five covered bridges in Yueshan Village, it gets its name from the cloud-like spray that rises from the waterfall under the bridge. The bridge is a woven timber arch-beam bridge, and it runs in a north-south direction. It is 8 meters long, 3 meters wide, and has a span of 7.5 meters. The bridge has a hip and gable roof with upturned double-eave, covered with small grey tiles.

步蟾桥

浙江省庆元县举水乡月山村，明永乐（1403—1424 年）

1917 年重建。独孔石拱廊桥，长 50 米、宽 5 米、高 8 米、跨径 16.6 米，十八开间。桥面铺条石块石，两侧设木制鳞叠护板，桥顶五脊四角挑檐，三间阁楼中间略大。正中为八角藻井和雕花垂柱。步蟾桥上游 30 米溪水中有一块巨石似蟾蜍，古人以此石为趣，为廊桥取名"步蟾"。属于处州廊桥，为全国重点文物保护单位。

Buchan Bridge

Yueshan Village, Jushui Township, Qingyuan County, Zhejiang Province, built during 1403-1424 AD.

The present Buchan Bridge was rebuilt in 1917 AD. The single-span covered bridge has a stone arch that is 50 meters long, 5 meters wide and 8 meters high, with a span of 16.6 meters. Its gallery house has 18 bays. The deck bridge is covered by stones with multi-layer wooden awnings at each side. Its roof has five ridges, four corners, and overhanging eaves. Of its pavilion's three bays, the middle one is slightly larger than the others. Inside, there is an eight-panel sunken caisson ceiling, as well as columns decorated with carved flowers. There is a stone resembling a toad (*chanchu* in Chinese) in the stream 30 meters upstream of the bridge, so the ancient people named the bridge Buchan Bridge as a result. Buchan Bridge is classified as Chuzhou Covered Bridges, which have been listed as a major historical and cultural sites protected at the national level.

刘宅桥

浙江省泰顺县三魁镇刘宅村，明永乐三年（1405 年）

古名仙洞虹桥。清康熙（1662—1722 年）、清乾隆（1736—1795 年）及清代晚期整修。殿宇式木平廊桥，长 24.8 米、宽 6.15 米、跨径 9.2 米，八开间。廊屋正脊两龙对视火舌宝珠，有镇水压财意趣。两层阁楼由扶梯连通，下层供通行，上层辟庙观。《魁峰高阳刘氏洞下桥记》记，修建仙洞虹桥"一为高阳本境风水之系，二为往来负任担荷之便，三为经商过客休息之所，四为秋七迎福康乐之会"。属于泰顺廊桥，为全国重点文物保护单位。

Liuzhai Bridge

Liuzhai Village, Sankui Town, Taishun County, Zhejiang Province, built in 1405 AD.

Originally known as the Xiandong Hongqiao Bridge, it was renovated during the reigns of Emperor Kangxi (1662-1722 AD), Emperor Qianlong (1736-1795 AD), and the late Qing Dynasty. The palace-style timber beam covered bridge is 24.8 meters long, 6.15 meters wide, and has a span of 9.2 meters. Its gallery house has 8 bays. There are carvings of two dragons eying a flaming jewel on the ridge of the gallery house's roof, with the associated significance of protecting the bridge from flooding. The gallery house has two levels: the first for people to walk through, and the upper level serves as a shrine. According to a travel journal, this bridge has four primary functions, firstly to promote positive *fengshui*, secondly to serve as a passageway for porters, thirdly as a place for travelers and merchants to rest, and fourthly as the site for autumnal festival gatherings. Liuzhai Bridge is classified as Taishun Covered Bridges, which have been listed as a major historical and cultural sites protected at the national level.

明代 1368—1644 年

仙居桥

浙江省泰顺县罗阳镇仙居村，明景泰四年（1453年）

贯木叠插别压式木拱廊桥，由泰顺知县郭显宗倡建，连通府衙至温州的要道。明成化十九年（1483年）水毁，明弘治四年（1491年）知县范勉筹资重建。明嘉靖三十年（1551年）倒塌，明嘉靖四十二年（1563年）知县区益多方募捐在原址重建。清康熙十二年（1673年）正月，村众集资重建。长41.83米、宽4.89米、高12.6米、跨径34.14米，十八开间。属于泰顺廊桥，为全国重点文物保护单位。

Xianju Bridge

Xianju Village, Luoyang Town, Taishun County, Zhejiang Province, built in 1453 AD.

This woven timber arch-beam covered bridge was built by Guo Xianzong, the magistrate of Taishun County, to connect the government office to Wenzhou. The bridge was destroyed by flood in 1483 AD. In 1491 AD, county magistrate Fan Mian raised money to rebuild it. Then, the bridge collapsed in 1551 AD and was rebuilt in 1563 AD with the money raised by Ou Yi, the county magistrate. In 1673 AD, villagers raised funds to reconstruct this bridge. Now the bridge is 41.83 meters long, 4.89 meters wide, 12.6 meters high, and has a span of 34.14 meters. Its gallery house has 18 bays. Xianju Bridge is classified as Taishun Covered Bridges, which have been listed as a major historical and cultural sites protected at the national level.

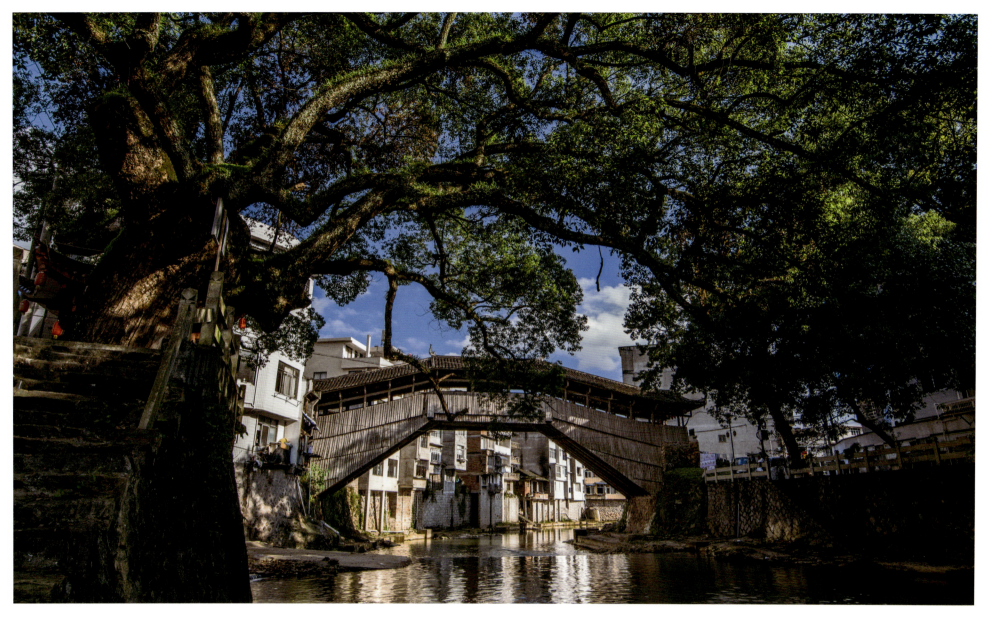

薛宅桥

浙江省泰顺县三魁镇薛外村锦溪，明正德七年（1512年）

　　古称锦溪桥。叠梁木拱廊桥，长51米、宽5.1米、高10.5米、跨径29米，十五开间，桥面拱矢斜度较大。明万历七年（1579年）突发山洪，薛宅桥被冲毁。清咸丰六年（1856年）复建。2016年受台风"莫兰蒂"影响，薛宅桥被完全冲毁，次年复建。属于泰顺廊桥，为全国重点文物保护单位。

Xuezhai Bridge

Jinxi Creek, Xuewai Village, Sankui Town, Taishun County, Zhejiang Province, built in 1512 AD.

It was named Jinxi Bridge in ancient times. It is a woven timber arch-beam covered bridge. It is 51 meters long, 5.1 meters wide, 10.5 meters high, and has a span of 29 meters. Its gallery house has 15 bays. The bridge arch rises at a steep angle. In 1579 AD, the bridge was destroyed by a flood and reconstructed in 1856 AD. Affected by Typhoon Meranti in 2016, Xuezhai Bridge was damaged, and was repaired the following year. Xuezhai Bridge is classified as Taishun Covered Bridges, which have been listed as a major historical and cultural sites protected at the national level.

登云桥

浙江省泰顺县罗阳镇，明正德（1506—1521 年）

原名镇南桥。始建于明正德（1506—1521 年）年间，由知县刘桐使用官银主持修建。位于泰顺县罗阳镇南门外泰寿溪，连通西南进出古道，也是往返福建省寿宁县要道。明万历（1573—1620 年）年间重建，更名为登云桥。一墩两孔伸臂式木拱廊桥，长 40 米、宽 5.5 米，两孔跨径共 25 米，十二开间。为省级文物保护单位。

Dengyun Bridge

Luoyang Town, Taishun County, Zhejiang Province, built during 1506-1521 AD.

Originally known as Zhennan Bridge. It was built by the decree of county magistrate Liu Tong with government funding. Crossing the Taishou Creek outside the south gate of Taishun County's Luoyang Town, the Dengyun Bridge not only connected the county with the ancient roads that led to southwest, it also served as an important passageway to Fujian's Shouning County. It was rebuilt during 1573-1620 AD, and was renamed Dengyun Bridge. The bridge has one pier and two spans and is a timber cantilever arch bridge. It is 40 meters long, 5.5 meters wide, and the total span of the two holes is 25 meters. Its gallery house has 12 bays. It has been listed as a historical and cultural sites protected at the provincial level.

溪东桥

浙江省泰顺县泗溪镇白粉墙村，明隆庆四年（1570年）

溪东桥与北涧桥相隔一里，互称姐妹桥。清乾隆十年（1745年）重建，清道光十年（1830年）修缮。长41.7米、宽4.86米、高10.35米、跨径25.7米，十五开间。属于泰顺廊桥，为全国重点文物保护单位。

Xidong Bridge

Baifenqiang Village, Sixi Town, Taishun County, Zhejiang Province, built in 1570 AD.

Xidong Bridge and Beijian Bridge are only 500 meters apart, and they are called sister bridges. Xidong Bridge was reconstructed in 1745 AD and repaired in 1830 AD. It is 41.7 meters long, 4.86 meters wide, 10.35 meters high, and has a span of 25.7 meters. Its gallery house has 15 bays. Xidong Bridge is classified as Taishu Covered Bridges, which have been listed as a major historical and cultural sites protected at the national level.

飞云桥

福建省寿宁县鳌阳镇，明天顺七年（1463 年）

曾名步云桥、后墩桥，县丞（副县长）李贞、乡绅吴永忠募建。清嘉庆二十三年（1818 年）、清光绪二年（1876 年）重修。1938 年修葺，1995 年修缮。两端桥堍用条石砌筑，长 29.2 米、宽 5.3 米、跨径 18.8 米，十三开间。东南与西北走向，双坡顶中间升出歇山顶小阁楼。

Feiyun Bridge

Aoyang Town, Shouning County, Fujian Province, built in 1463 AD.

The bridge is also known as Buyun Bridge and Houdun Bridge. Li Zhen, the assistant county magistrate, and Wu Yongzhong, a member of the local gentry, raised money for the construction of the bridge. In 1818 AD and 1876 AD, the bridge was renovated. It was also renovated in 1938 AD and 1995. The two ends of the bridge are made of stone. Its length is 29.2 meters, and its width is 5.3 meters. Its span is 18.8 meters and its gallery house has 13 bays. The bridge is oriented from the southeast to the northwest. Its roof has two slopes. In the middle, there is a small pavilion with a hip and gable roof.

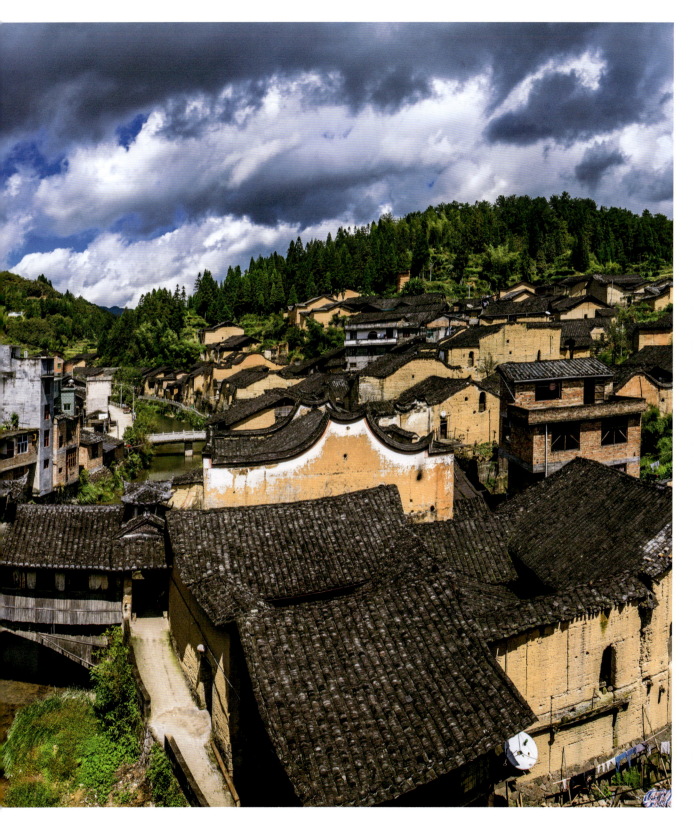

三仙桥

福建省周宁县纯池镇禾溪村，明成化三年（1467年）

　　曾名澄明桥、三顶桥，因供奉杨、柳、倪三位仙姑而改名。穿斗式架构，单孔亭阁式木拱廊桥，长18.4米、宽5.4米、跨径19米，七开间。桥面铺木板，桥端建门亭，桥顶建中大侧小四角挑檐阁楼。1917年，建桥匠师许顺金主持重建。1949年后两次大修。三仙桥是村民沟通往来、议事休闲、粘贴布告、物品买卖场所。为县级文物保护单位。民间说书艺人常在廊桥内为村民表演。

Sanxian Bridge

Hexi Village, Chunchi Town, Zhouning County, Fujian Province, built in 1467 AD.

Previously, it was called Chengming Bridge and Sanding Bridge, but its name was changed to honor the three female immortals—Yang, Liu, and Ni. It is a timber frame arch covered bridge. Its gallery house is a *chuandou* style structure and has 7 bays. It is 18.4 meters long, 5.4 meters wide, and has a span of 19 meters. Its deck is covered with timber boards, a gate pavilion is installed at the end of the bridge. The gallery house is tall in the center and smaller at the sides, and is covered by a four cornered roof with overhanging eaves. Xu Shunjin, a master bridge builder, presided over the reconstruction of the bridge in 1917 AD. After 1949, the bridge underwent two major renovations. Sanxian Bridge is a place for villagers to communicate and relax, post announcements, and buy and sell goods. It has been listed as a historical and cultural sites protected at the county level. Traditional storytellers often perform for villagers on the covered bridge.

明代 1368—1644年

老人桥

福建省福鼎市管阳镇西阳村,明正德(1506—1521年)

清光绪(1875—1908年)年间《乡土志》记:"邱阜,瓦洋人,有齿德,为遐迩排难纠纷者数十年。有某妇悍甚,小忿涉讼。(邱)阜劝谕弗听,自耻德薄,赴水死。闾里感其诚,建桥设主以祀。至今呼为老人桥云。"伸臂式木拱廊桥,长30.8米、宽4.8米、高8米。由135根贯木设置上中下三层分为五组,形成互为依托、衔接紧密、稳固支撑的梁架结构。

Laoren Bridge

Xiyang Village, Guanyang Town, Fuding, Fujian Province, built during 1506-1521 AD.

A *Local Chronicle* from the Qing Dynasty's Guangxu (1875-1908 AD) period records that "Qiu Fu, a man of Wayang, was a person of venerable age and eminent virtue. For over ten years he had presided over difficult cases from near and far. There was a shrewish woman who then pursued a lawsuit over a small dispute. Qiu Fu did not succeed in admonishing her, so he was ashamed of his limited virtue and drowned himself. The people in the area were moved by his virtue and built the bridge as a tribute to him, and up to the present it has been known as Laoren Bridge." The timber cantilever arch covered bridge is 30.8 meters long, 4.8 meters wide, and 8 meters high. Three stories composed of 135 timbers are divided into five groups, forming an interdependent, tight, and stable supporting beam-frame structure.

金朱桥

福建省福鼎市管阳镇金钗溪村,明代
(1368—1644年)

  明代始建,清乾隆(1736—1795年)、清咸丰(1851—1861年)年间重修。单孔石拱木结构廊桥,东西走向,长28.24米、宽4.27米、高4.2米,十一开间,竖柱46根。桥东端遗存"大清乾隆二十年(1755年)""大清咸丰五年(1855年)"重修金朱桥纪事碑各一方。原为木梁廊桥,清乾隆二十年(1755年),族首朱肇衍公等筹资改建为石拱廊桥,取金钗溪与朱姓合一之意,取名"金朱桥"。

Jinzhu Bridge

Jinchaixi Village, Guanyang Town, Fuding, Fujian Province, built during 1368-1644 AD.

The bridge was originally constructed during 1368-1644 AD and was rebuilt sometime between 1736 AD and 1795 AD, as well as sometime between 1851 AD and 1861 AD. It is a timber covered bridge with a stone arch and a single span. It is 28.24 meters long, 4.27 meters wide and 4.2 meters high. Its gallery house has 11 bays and is oriented in an east-west direction. At the eastern end of the bridge, steles dedicated to the bridge dating from "The Second Decade of Emperor Qianlong of the Qing Dynasty" (1755 AD) and "The Fifth Year of the Emperor Xianfeng of the Qing Dynasty" (1855 AD) are installed. Originally it was a wooden bridge. Later, in 1755 AD, Zhu Zhaoyan, the lineage head, raised funds to rebuild it as a stone arch bridge and named it Jinzhu Bridge, based on the shared relationship between the Jinchai Creek and the Zhu lineage.

大宝桥

福建省寿宁县坑底乡小东村,明代（1368—1644年）

曾名小东桥,长44.5米、宽4.6米、跨径33米,十九开间,挑檐悬山顶覆小青瓦。因洪水期水面高、流速快,大宝桥拱跨弧度很大,两端桥堍用大块坚石砌筑,并在河水主峰头一侧桥堍建造一座船首形石墩。廊内设木凳、木板床。清光绪四年（1878年）重建。为省级文物保护单位。

Dabao Bridge

Xiaodong Village, Kengdi Township, Shouning County, Fujian Province, built during 1368-1644 AD.

Also known as Xiaodong Bridge, it was rebuilt in 1878 AD. It is 44.5 meters long, 4.6 meters wide, and has a span of 33 meters. Its gallery house has 19 bays. Its two-slope overhanging gable roof has extended eaves and is covered with small grey tiles. Because of the speed and force of sudden floods here, the bridge's arch is built with a steep angle of incline, the two sides of the bridge use large stone blocks, and the bridge pier is shaped as the bow of a ship. The bridge has been listed as a historical and cultural sites protected at the provincial level.

明代 1368—1644 年

金造桥

福建省屏南县棠口镇漈头村,明代(1368—1644年)

清乾隆十四年(1749年)重建。清嘉庆十年(1805年)焚毁,清嘉庆十五年(1810年)贡生张永衢募捐重建。1948年再次重建。全木结构伸臂式独孔廊桥,长41.7米、宽4.8米、跨径32.5米。廊屋十五间,悬山挑檐顶覆小青瓦。金造桥处在新修水电站淹没区,遂于2005年迁至距原址数公里外国家级森林保护区内。

Jinzao Bridge

Jitou Village, Tangkou Town, Pingnan County, Fujian Province, built during 1368-1644 AD.

The bridge was rebuilt in 1749 AD. In 1805 AD, the bridge burned down, and later, in 1810 AD, it was restored with the help of Zhang Yongqu, who raised funds for the project. In 1948 AD, the bridge was reconstruction again. It is a timber-frame, single-span cantilever covered bridge. It is 41.7 meters long, 4.8 meters wide, and has a span of 32.5 meters. Its gallery house has 15 bays, and its overhanging eaves are covered with small grey tiles. In 2005, the bridge was relocated to a national forest reserve several kilometers away from its original site due to the construction of a hydropower station.

腾云桥

福建省建瓯市玉山镇敷锡村，明洪武二年（1369年）

曾名敷锡桥，石砌叠木桥墩、单拱圆木双层平搭伸梁式廊桥，长54米、宽5米、高7.6米、跨径16米。《腾云桥记》载："据《八闽通志》、清《建宁府志》记载，敷锡桥明洪武二年（1369年）由里人黄任波筹建。清嘉庆十七年（1812年）敷锡詹氏子孙42人为首筹资重建为单拱木架伸臂廊桥，改名腾云桥。因桥屋瓦片、桥面、雨披等多处破损，2008年整修。"桥头遗留雍正三年（1725年）《严禁砍伐树木碑》一方。

Tengyun Bridge

Fuxi Village, Yushan Town, Jian'ou, Fujian Province, built in 1369 AD.

Originally named Fuxi Bridge. Tengyun Bridge has piers composed of stone masonry and stacked timbers. It is formed with logs and is a two-story cantilever covered bridge with a single arch. It is 54 meters long, 5 meters wide and 7.6 meters high. It has a span of 16 meters. It is recorded in *Records of the Tengyun Bridge* that, "As it is stated in the *History of Fujian* and the Qing Dynasty *History of Jianning*, Fuxi Bridge, a timber arch covered bridge, was built by Huang Renbo and other villagers in the second year of the Emperor Hongwu period in the Ming Dynasty (1369 AD). It was reconstructed as a timber cantilever covered bridge with a single span in the 17th year of the Emperor Jiaqing period in the Qing Dynasty (1812 AD) by 42 members of the Zhan lineage, at which time it was renamed the Tengyun Bridge. The bridge was renovated in 2008 because its tiles, deck, and awnings had been worn out." A *Prohibition of Logging* stele erected in 1725 AD stands at the entrance to the bridge.

镇安桥

福建省浦城县临江镇，明洪武十二年（1379年）

《镇安桥修复记》载："古有'川无梁，政不修'之说。古贤者云'余邑之胜以山，山之胜以浦，浦之胜以桥'。闽中桥梁巨丽，桥上架屋翼翼楚楚，无处不堪图画，镇安桥如是矣。"原名临江桥，明正统十一年（1446年）更名为镇安桥。桥堡式廊桥横跨临江溪，东西走向，四墩三孔，叠木平梁辅以贯木八字支撑。桥屋二十间，庑殿顶。长96.5米、宽3.6米，两端石砌台阶21级，引道长5米，旁立石栏，东西桥头砖砌拱门，眉刻"镇安保障"。2009年焚毁，2012年重建。

Zhen'an Bridge

Linjiang Town, Pucheng County, Fujian Province, built in 1379 AD.

As it states in the *Restoration of Zhen'an Bridge*, "In the past there was the saying, 'A creek not crossed (by a bridge) shows that rule has not been achieved.' Ancient sages remarked that 'mountains are the pride of our area, rivers are the pride of mountains, and bridges are the pride of rivers.' Bridges of Fujian are magnificent and everywhere boast distinctive pavilions, with no place less wondrous than a painting. Zhen'an Bridge is one such place." Formerly named Linjiang Bridge, it was renamed Zhen'an Bridge in 1446 AD. This covered bridge spans the Linjiang River from east to west and has four piers and three spans. Its woven timber beams are supported by *bazi* bracing. Its gallery house has 20 bays and is 96.5 meters long and 3.6 meters wide. It is covered by a hipped roof. At both ends are 21 stone steps and a 5 meters approach flanked by a stone wall. There are also archways at both ends inscribed with the words "Zhen'an Bridge Protector". The bridge was destroyed in a fire in 2009 and was rebuilt in 2012.

明代 1368—1644年

五福桥

福建省松溪县渭田镇渭田溪，明永乐（1403—1424年）

曾名八岭桥，长108米、宽5.2米、高12米，四墩五孔，东西走向，横跨渭田溪。据《尚书》"长寿、富贵、康宁、好德、善终"为五福而定桥名。《重修五福桥记》载："清光绪二十七年（1901年）端午，狂涛怒吼冲圮两墩。逾二年各界人士募捐重建，清光绪三十四年（1908年）竣工。桥如旧制。"墩尖雕琢鹰鸦头嘴，桥北两端桥门为牌坊式三层挑角结构。正中建重檐翘角亭阁，题曰"赛濠观"。枋板绘《三国演义》《东周列国志》故事。

Wufu Bridge

over Weitian Creek at Weitian Town, Songxi County, Fujian Province, built during 1403-1424 AD.

Originally named Baling Bridge, it is 108 meters long, 5.2 meters wide, and 12 meters high and spans the Weitian Creek from east to west. It has four piers and five spans. Its present name comes from *The Book of History* (one of the five classics of ancient Chinese literature), which lists five blessings for "longevity, affluence, health, benevolence, and a natural death". As *The Reconstruction of Wufu Bridge* states, "During the Dragon Boat Festival in the 27th year of the Emperor Guangxu period of the Qing Dynasty (1901 AD), the roaring river toppled down two bridge piers. Two years later, people from all walks of life collected money to rebuild the bridge, which was restored in the 34th year of the Emperor Guangxu period of the Qing Dynasty (1908 AD)." The tip of the pier is carved in the shape of the beak of an eagle or crow. At the bridge's north and at its gateways are decorative three-story archways with projecting corners. In the center of the bridge, there is a pavilion with multiple eaves and upturned corners, called the Saihao Temple. Beams in the bridge are painted with scenes from *Romance of the Three Kingdoms* and *Chronicles of the Eastern Zhou Dynasty's Kingdoms*.

花桥

福建省政和县杨源乡坂头村，明正德六年（1511年）

南北走向，单孔石拱楼阁式廊桥，长38米、宽8米、跨径12.2米，十三开间。抬梁穿斗式结构，三重檐歇山顶五层飞檐翘角，中亭和两端建阁楼，犹如盛开的莲花，由此得名。清康熙（1662—1722年）、清道光（1821—1850年）、清咸丰（1851—1861年）年间、1914年、1982年重修。常来上香的妇女祈祷远在他乡打工的晚辈健康平安、财进事成。当时专供女人行走的狭窄通道，至今仍有年老妇女通行。

Huaqiao Bridge

Bantou Village, Yangyuan Township, Zhenghe County, Fujian Province, built in 1511 AD.

Running from north to south, this stone arch pavilion covered bridge has a single span. It is 38 meters long, 8 meters wide, and has a span of 12.2 meters. The gallery house has 13 bays and is a combined *tailiang* and *chuandou* style structure. It has a five story gallery house with a triple-eave hip and gable roof with upturned eaves and winged corners. There is a pagoda in the center and pavilions built on each side. This bridge appears like a blooming lotus flower, and its name refers to this resemblance. The bridge was rebuilt several times during the reigns of Emperor Kangxi (1662-1722 AD), Emperor Daoguang (1821-1850 AD), and Emperor Xianfeng (1851-1861 AD) of the Qing Dynasty, as well as in 1914 AD and 1982. Women often come here to burn incense and pray for health, safety, prosperity, and success of the younger generations who work far away from home. A narrow passageway on the bridge was once provided for the exclusive use of women, and it is still used by a few of the elderly women in the village today.

步月桥

福建省建瓯市吉阳镇玉溪村，明正德十四年（1519年）

现桥为明正德十四年（1519年）重建。乡民在中秋节将象征"吉祥、添丁"的红、白灯笼挂在步月桥廊，看上别家灯笼可摘走，"摘一"次年须"还六"民俗延续至今。一墩两孔复合叠梁木平梁廊桥，长128米、宽6米、高7米，四十二开间。清乾隆二十六年（1761年），商户张士华雇工在玉溪河放木失控将步月桥撞塌，赔偿铜钱七百万修复。清道光五年（1825年），士绅葛军操捐钱粮修缮。清光绪十九年（1893年），黄声过出资大修。1998年，洪水淘空墩基，桥体倾斜。妇女耕山队长葛兰妹带头捐款，百姓积极响应，政府筹资90万元重建。2019年1月31日，步月桥因失火焚毁，2020年时完成重建。

Buyue Bridge

Yuxi Village, Jiyang Town, Jian'ou, Fujian Province, built in 1519 AD.

The existing bridge was rebuilt in 1519 AD. During the Mid-Autumn Lantern Festival, there are always red and white lanterns placed in the Buyue Bridge's gallery house, used to pray for happiness and for the birth of children. Anyone can take his or her favorite lantern back home. The next year, however, one has to hang six times the number of lanterns that were taken the previous year. This tradition has been passed on to the present day. Buyue Bridge has one pier and two spans. It is a compound woven timber beam and multi-span, simply supported timber beam covered bridge. Its gallery house has 42 bays, and it is 128 meters long, 6 meters wide, and 7 meters high. In 1761 AD, an employee of the merchant Zhang Shihua lost control of the timber he was transporting along the Yuxi River, destroying Buyue Bridge. Zhang then paid seven million copper coins to restore the bridge. In 1825 AD, a member of the local gentry, Ge Juncao, donated money and food to repair the bridge. Major repairs were completed again on the bridge in 1893 AD with the use of a large donation by Huang Sheng'e. In 1998, the flood scoured the foundations of the piers, causing the bridge to tilt. In response, Ge Lanmei, who led the formation of a renowned all-female ploughing team in 1963, set an example again by donating to rebuild the bridge, and many local villagers followed in kind. This, together with 900,000 yuan in government funding, allowed the bridge to be rebuilt. On January 31, 2019, the bridge was destroyed by fire and was rebuilt in 2020.

明代 1368—1644年

承安桥

福建省光泽县鸾凤乡油溪村，明万历（1573—1620年）

农历七月初六子夜，方圆数十里乡众会集聚于承安桥，祈求有情人终成眷属，夫妻恩爱。又名七星桥、夫妻桥。1942年毁于大火，次年重建。三墩四孔木结构廊桥，长60米、宽6.5米、高7米。桥面铺石板和鹅卵石，两侧安置挡雨板。村里妇女逢修桥开工，会聚到桥旁祈祷顺利圆满。

Cheng'an Bridge

Youxi Village, Luanfeng Township, Guangze County, Fujian Province, built during 1573-1620 AD.

Every year during the night of the sixth day of the seventh lunar month, villagers from surrounding villages gather at the Cheng'an Bridge to pray that lovers will form honorable households and that husbands and wives will find love and comfort. Also named Qixing Bridge and Fuqi Bridge, it was destroyed in 1942 AD by a fire accidentally. It was rebuilt the following year. The bridge has three piers and four spans. It is a timber frame bridge that is 60 meters long, 6.5 meters wide, and 7 meters high. The bridge deck is covered by stone slabs and cobblestones. Both sides are protected by awnings to keep out the rain. Traditionally, when repairs are made on the bridge, the village's women gather to pray that the project be smooth and successful.

兴龙桥

福建省建瓯市迪口镇可建村,明代(1368—1644年)

又名李溪厝桥。廊架正梁遗留"大明崇祯柒年(1634年)岁运甲戌孟冬玖月十八旦辛未寅时良辰重新建造""时维大清道光肆年(1824年)甲申岁拾月二辛未日午时升梁重建"墨迹。兴龙桥构成实用简洁,八字木拱居中、石台复合支撑木平梁。全木结构廊桥,南北走向,长35米、宽4米、高9.6米、单孔跨径12.7米,十二开间,穿斗式结构,单脊双坡硬山顶覆小青瓦。为市级文物保护单位。

Xinglong Bridge

Kejian Village, Dikou Town, Jian'ou, Fujian Province, built during 1368-1644 AD.

Xinglong Bridge is also named Lixicuo Bridge. Characters written on its main beam state, "Rebuilt during *yinshi* (three a.m. to five a.m.) on the eighteenth day of the ninth lunar month in the seventh year of the Emperor Chongzhen period in the Ming Dynasty (1634 AD)" and "Rebuilt during *wushi* (eleven a.m. to one p.m.) on the second day of the tenth lunar month in the fourth year of the Emperor Daoguang period in the Qing Dynasty (1824 AD)." The structure of Xinglong Bridge is practical and concise—it has an arch formed by *bazi* bracing in its center, and its compound stone abutments support the bridge's horizontal timber beams. The north-south timber frame covered bridge is 35 meters long, 4 meters wide, 9.6 meters high, and has a span of 12.7 meters. Its gallery house has 12 bays and is a *chuandou* style structure covered by a single-ridge, two-slope flush gable roof topped by small grey tiles. The bridge has been listed as a historical and cultural sites protected at the municipal level.

集瑞桥

福建省建瓯市南雅镇集瑞村，明代（1368—1644年）

集瑞桥由大小两座廊桥组成，"母子廊桥"合成一体，为国内仅有。《嘉靖建宁府志》记载："集瑞桥成化二年（1466年）重建，木梁，构亭七楹。"清咸丰三年（1853年）整修。大桥建于明早期，长27米、宽5米、跨径8米，九开间，四柱九檩抬梁式全木结构，硬山顶下置遮雨板。小桥建于清中期，长18.5米、宽1.2米，四开间，单坡顶覆小青瓦。

Jirui Bridge

Jirui Village, Nanya Town, Jian'ou, Fujian Province, built during 1368-1644 AD.

Jirui Bridge consists of two covered bridges, large and small, forming a "Mother and Child Covered Bridge" integrated as one, which is the only one in China. As the *History of Jianning in the Emperor Jiajing Period* states, "Jirui Bridge, was reconstructed in 1466 AD and is made of timber beams and a pavilion with seven columns." It was rebuilt in 1853 AD. The larger of the two bridges was built in the early Ming Dynasty. It is 27 meters long, 5 meters wide, and has a span of 8 meters. Its gallery house has 9 bays. It is a *tailiang* style structure with four columns and nine purlins. It is covered by a flush gable roof, with awnings installed to keep off the rain. The smaller bridge was built in the mid Qing Dynasty. It is 18.5 meters long, 1.2 meters wide, and has a gallery house with 4 bays. Its single-slope roof is covered by small grey tiles.

永隆桥

福建省连城县莒溪镇壁洲村，明洪武二十年（1387年）

　　南北走向、四孔五跨、石墩平梁木结构廊桥，长85米、宽6米、高7.5米。桥北端建有重檐歇山顶阁楼，桥中、桥尾南端建有歇山顶矮阁。穿斗式架构，花岗岩桥墩上纵横叠木七层组成主体支撑，桥面铺满由河床捞取的鹅卵石，硬山式覆小青瓦，桥侧设置双层挡风薄木护板。六百余年未受损毁，是闽西极具文物价值的古代建筑标本，被列为省级文物保护单位。

Yonglong Bridge

Bizhou Village, Juxi Town, Liancheng County, Fujian Province, built in 1387 AD.

Running from south to north, the bridge has four piers and five spans. It is a multi-span simply supported timber beam covered bridge with stone piers. It is 85 meters long, 6 meters wide, 7.5 meters high, and is a *chuandou* style structure. On the north side of the bridge is a pavilion building with a multiple-eave hip and gable roof. In the center and southern end of the bridge, small pavilions also covered with hip and gable roofs. Seven layers of criss-crossed logs form the main bracing structure, placed upon the bridge's granite piers. The bridge deck is covered with cobblestones gathered from the riverbed. The gallery house is covered by a flush gable roof, topped with small grey tiles, and double-layer protective skirts made of thin wood run alongside the bridge, blocking the wind. For over 600 years, the bridge has not become damaged or worn down. It is an ancient architectural specimen in western Fujian with significant cultural value. The bridge has been listed as a historical and cultural sites protected at the provincial level.

云龙桥

福建省连城县罗坊乡下罗村口青岩河，明崇祯七年（1634年）

东西走向，石墩圆木叠梁、全木结构亭阁式廊桥，长81米、宽5米、高20米。廊桥正中偏西建有双层六角攒尖顶魁星楼，两端安设高挑檐牌楼。桥型巍峨雄奇犹如蛟龙，故名。为省级文物保护单位。每年正月十五下午一点半，罗坊乡云龙桥下青岩河会准时上演客家人呼啸"走古事"数万人助威的盛大狂欢。七族各选勇敢男童上扮主官，下扮护将。

Yunlong Bridge

Qingyan River at Xialuo Village, Luofang Township, Liancheng County, Fujian Province, built in 1634 AD.

Running from east to west, it is a pavilion-style combined log beam covered bridge with stone piers. It is 81 meters long, 5 meters wide, and 20 meters high. Just to the west of the center of the bridge is a two-story, six-sided pyramidal Kuixing Tower (*kuixing* is the Taoist god of examinations) with a pyramidal roof. Both ends of the bridge have decorative archways with tall protruding eaves. The bridge's form is towering and bold, like a dragon, and it is named because of this resemblance. It has been listed as a historical and cultural sites protected at the provincial level. Every year at 1:30 p.m. on the 15th day of the first lunar month, villagers will follow the Hakka Nationality's tradition of hosting a large scale festival and performing a pageant, which is conducted through the participation of thousands of people. Seven lineages each select brave boys who are costumed as main characters who stand on the upper part of a platform and as guards in the lower part of the platform.

见龙桥

福建省尤溪县新阳镇双鲤村，明正统元年（1436年）

双鲤村因见龙桥下两块巨石形如鲤鱼而得名。全木结构单孔廊桥，东西走向，长30米、宽5米、高4米，单孔跨径14米，八开间，悬山顶。桥面由圆木三层纵横叠架，两侧安置遮阳板、栏杆、长条凳。1924年，里人卢兴邦为造福桑梓出资重修。

Jianlong Bridge

Shuangli Village, Xinyang Town, Youxi County, Fujian Province, built in 1436 AD.

Under the Jianlong Bridge, there are two giant stones that resemble two carp fish, and this is what the village is named after. Running from east to west, this single-span timber frame covered bridge is 30 meters long, 5 meters wide, 4 meters high, and has a span of 14 meters. Its gallery house has 8 bays and an overhanging gable roof. The bridge deck is supported by three levels of stacked criss-crossed logs. Railing and benches are installed on both sides of the bridge. In 1924 AD, Lu Xingbang contributed funds for the bridge's reconstruction.

神仙桥

福建省宁化县曹坊镇滑石村，明景泰元年（1450年）至明天顺四年（1460年）

又名温孙桥、解放桥。四墩五孔全木结构廊桥，长80余米、宽6米、高6.2米，二十一开间。船首形石筑桥墩迎水面呈雀喙状，墩台上圆木纵横交错七层或十层承托木梁。桥廊中间安设神龛，遮雨板下侧设护栏、长凳。单脊双坡顶桥头建悬山顶重檐小望阁。神仙桥为明代始建原物，是宁化县遗存最久远的大型廊桥。古为泰宁、建宁、宁化等县通往汀州府"盐米古道"的重要津梁。

Shenxian Bridge

Huashi Village, Caofang Town, Ninghua County, Fujian Province, built during 1450-1460 AD.

Also known as Wensun Bridge and Jiefang Bridge, the bridge has four piers and five spans. It is a timber frame covered bridge that is over 80 meters long, 6 meters wide, and 6.2 meters high. Its gallery house has 21 bays. The side of its stone pier facing upstream is shaped in the form of a sparrow's beak. On top of the stone pier are seven or ten layers of criss-crossing logs that support the bridge's beams. The middle of the bridge has a shrine, with an awning to block the rain above and a protective railing below. The bridge has a single-ridge double-slope roof, and at its ends there are small viewing pavilions with multiple-eaves and overhanging gables. As a well-preserved bridge built in the Ming Dynasty (1368-1644 AD), Shenxian Bridge is the oldest large-scale covered bridge in Ninghua County. In ancient times, it served the important "Ancient Salt Grain Passageway" that connected Taining, Jianning, and Ninghua counties to Tingzhou Prefecture.

流泗桥

福建省大田县桃源镇兰玉村，明成化（1465—1487年）

清康熙（1662—1722年）年间、1912—1949年间整修。一墩两孔全木结构廊桥，东西走向，长42.2米、宽4.5米、高5米，两门厅十开间，两旁设有鹅颈椅，外搭遮雨篷。船首形条石桥墩迎水面呈鸟喙状，其上六层圆木交叉支托横木平梁，桥面使用长条木板铺设。单脊三重檐悬山顶，中脊安置翘尾龙抢宝葫芦，各檐角安放"水花"雕塑。

Liusi Bridge

Lanyu Village, Taoyuan Town, Datian County, Fujian Province, built during 1465-1487 AD.

This bridge was overhauled between 1662-1722 AD and 1912-1949 AD. It has one pier and two spans and runs from east to west. The bridge is 42.2 meters long, 4.5 meters wide, and 5 meters high. It has two halls and its gallery house has 10 bays. There are benches on both sides and awnings that protect the bridge. The side of the stone pier facing upstream is shaped in the form of a sparrow's beak, and above this are six intersecting layers of logs that support the horizontal bridge beams. The bridge deck is covered with long timber boards. The bridge is covered by a single-ridge overhanging gable roof with three eaves. In the center of the ridge is a dragon with an upturned tail, grabbing a gourd-shaped treasure. The ends of all the eaves are decorated by carvings of splashing water.

会清桥

福建省永安市贡川镇集凤村,明天启六年(1626年)

沙溪、胡贡溪在廊桥下交汇,清浊分明,浊水多被清流融会,因此得名会清桥。清道光二十年(1840年)大修。南北走向,两墩三孔,长41米、宽7米、高8米,十一开间。两端建门楼,歇山顶桥亭。农历三月三,乡民祭拜水神,祈盼风调雨顺。屋檐下有泥塑彩绘,正脊"鱼吻"寓意防火镇水。为省级文物保护单位。

Huiqing Bridge

Jifeng Village, Gongchuan Town, Yongan, Fujian Province, built in 1626 AD.

The Shaxi Creek and Hugong Creek converge under this covered bridge, during which muddy water is purified by the larger-volume clean current. This is how the bridge got its name. The bridge was overhauled in 1840 AD. Running from north to south, it has two piers and three spans. It is 41 meters long, 7 meters wide, and 8 meters high. Its gallery house has 11 bays. Pavilions with hip and gable roofs, together with gateway arches, are built on both ends. On the third day of the third lunar month, villagers gather at the bridge to worship the god of the water and pray for good weather. There are clay sculptures and colorful paintings inside the bridge, and on the ridge, there is a sculpture of a fish, thought to offer protection against flooding and fires. It has been listed as a historical and cultural sites protected at the provincial level.

广济桥

福建省德化县春美乡双翰村，明嘉靖元年（1522年）

又名双翰下桥。连通永春县经德化县到大田县古官道。石基叠木伸臂式廊桥，长24米、宽5.5米、高6.5米，七开间。清顺治十四年（1657年）、清乾隆九年（1744年）水毁重建。1972年，旅居马来西亚华侨苏重仁、苏首相等人回乡祭祖，发起海外华侨同乡募捐集资，于1974年重修。为县级文物保护单位。

Guangji Bridge

Shuanghan Village, Chunmei Township, Dehua County, Fujian Province, built in 1522 AD.

Also known as Shuanghan Xiaqiao Bridge. Guangji Bridge connected a major ancient official road that linked Yongchun County to Datian County via Dehua County. The bridge is a timber cantilever covered bridge built with timbers stacked on top of its stone foundation. It is 24 meters long, 5.5 meters wide, and 6.5 meters high. Its gallery house has 7 bays. The bridge was damaged by floods and then rebuilt in both 1657 AD and 1744 AD. In 1972, overseas Chinese residents of Malaysia Su Chongren, Su Shouxiang, and others, returned to the village to pay respects to their ancestors. They then organized their fellow landsmen abroad to raise money to repair the bridge, leading to its renovation in 1974. The bridge has been listed as a historical and cultural sites protected at the county level.

乐寿桥

安徽省黄山市屯溪区奕棋镇占川村，明万历（1573—1620年）

又名关爷桥、关阳桥。按《论语》"智者乐，仁者寿"的寓意定桥名。木廊穿斗式廊桥，一墩两孔，长30米、宽5.6米，七开间。粗大圆木为梁，上面逐层铺木板、薄砖、细沙，桥面用麻石板铺设。亭阁式桥顶，中间高、两侧低，覆青杂瓦。桥廊靠溪水上游一面置木凳，供乡民交谈聚会歇息。清光绪三十二年（1906年）、1948年重修。为区级文物保护单位。

Leshou Bridge

Zhanchuan Village, Yiqi Town, Tunxi District, Huangshan, Anhui Province, built during 1573-1620 AD.

Also known as Guanye Bridge and Guanyang Bridge. Leshou Bridge was named after a saying from *the Analects of Confucius*—"The wise are joyful (*le*); the virtuous are long-lived (*shou*)." The one pier two span timber *chuandou* pavilion-style covered bridge is 30 meters long, 5.6 meters wide, and has a gallery house with 7 bays. Its beams are made of thick logs. On top of them are layers of timber boards, thin bricks, and fine sand. Its deck is covered by granite stone. It is taller in the middle and lower on either end. It is covered with assorted grey tiles. On the side of the bridge facing upstream, there are wooden benches that allow villagers to talk together and rest. The bridge was rebuilt in 1906 AD and 1948 AD. It has been listed as a historical and cultural sites protected at the district level.

明代 1368—1644年

云溪桥

安徽省休宁县岭南乡三溪村,明代(1368—1644 年)

独孔石拱砖石结构亭阁式廊桥,长 25 米、宽 3 米、高 12 米,拱跨 6 米。

Yunxi Bridge

Sanxi Village, Lingnan Township, Xiuning County, Anhui Province, built during 1368-1644 AD.

This single-span bridge has an arch made of stone and a structure built of bricks. It is a pavilion style covered bridge, and is 25 meters long, 3 meters wide and 12 meters high. It has a span of 6 meters.

三棵树桥

安徽省休宁县蓝田镇，明代（1368—1644 年）

三棵树桥，因旁侧三株近三百年树龄苦槠树得名。早名淙潭桥，两墩三孔，石拱单面敞轩式廊桥。清雍正（1723—1735 年）、咸丰（1851—1861 年）年间整修。桥头立有清乾隆四十五年（1780 年）徽州府正堂颁布的"严禁砍伐树木，严禁在夹溪河药鱼"石碑。

Sankeshu Bridge

Lantian Town, Xiuning County, Anhui Province, built during 1368-1644 AD.

Sankeshu Bridge is named after three castanopsis evergreen trees that are adjacent to the bridge and which are almost 300 years old. Originally called Congtan Bridge, this bridge has two piers and three spans. It is a stone arch bridge with one side of its pavilion structure exposed. It was renovated between 1723-1735 AD and 1851-1861 AD. In 1780 AD, the Huizhou prefectural government inscribed a stone stele at the entrance of the bridge warning that fishing and cutting down trees is prohibited.

通济桥

江西省婺源县思口镇思溪村,明代(1368—1644年)

一墩两孔平梁木结构廊桥,长20余米,桥墩前端尖锐如锋,当地俗称燕嘴。墩台立六角如来石刻尊柱,寓意镇水保民。桥廊奉大禹神,村民崇敬他为民生社稷操劳、一心治水的仁心善举。思溪村俞氏一族数百年前加入徽商行列并自成一脉,常有经商致富的人携资归乡兴建书院祠堂、建桥修路等。

Tongji Bridge

Sixi Village, Sikou Town, Wuyuan County, Jiangxi Province, built during 1368-1644 AD.

This flat beam timber covered bridge has one pier and two spans and is more than 20 meters long. The sides of the bridge piers that face upstream come to a sharp point, and local people call them "swallow beaks". The hexagonal piers are carved with the status of Buddhas, thought to protect local people from floods. The gallery house is dedicated to Da Yu (the third of the three Legendary emperors who created the Chinese state), in honor of his benevolent achievements in flood control. Hundreds of years ago, the Yu lineage (not surnamed the same Yu as "Da Yu") from Sixi Village joined the legendary Huizhou merchants and formed their own network. Wealthy merchants returned home with funds that they contributed to the construction of academies, ancestral halls, bridges, and roads.

泰新桥

广东省封开县平凤镇平岗村,明嘉靖十二年(1533年)

据《封川县志》记载,此桥"嘉靖十二年(1533年)邑人陈时用等募缘修建,长十余丈,阔一丈,上覆以亭"。桥廊正梁存"大清嘉庆十六年(1811年)岁次辛未十一月十七日壬辰日癸卯时东西社众缘信等重建"墨迹。长10.9米、宽3.4米,方形石柱桥墩,四根石柱一组共四排上托石梁。1987年冬修缮。

Taixin Bridge

Pinggang Village, Pingfeng Town, Fengkai County, Guangdong Province, built in 1533 AD.

As it is recorded in *The History of Fengchuan County*, "In 1533 AD, Chen Shiyong and other villagers collected donations to build the bridge, which was over 10 *zhang* long (about 33.3 meters) and 1 *zhang* wide (about 3.3 meters) with a pavilion on top." On the bridge's main beam, it is written that the bridge was rebuilt at *guimao* (5 a.m. to 7 a.m.) on the 17th day of the eleventh lunar month in the 16th year of the Emperor Jiaqing reign in the Qing Dynasty (1811 AD). Taixin Bridge is 10.9 meters long and 3.4 meters wide with square stone piers and four rows with four stone columns each supporting the bridge's stone beams. The bridge was renovated in the winter of 1987.

高桥

云南省腾冲市界头镇龙川江,明成化二年(1466 年)

两墩三孔木梁廊桥,长 35 米、宽 2 米、高 25 米,是桥墩最高的中国廊桥。龙川江发源于高黎贡山,在高桥峡谷骤然收拢,水流较大。据杜福广先生(1963 年出生,界头镇张家营村人)介绍:"雨季龙川江急流撞击高桥峡谷石壁,河谷沟崖石壁表面伤痕累累。老辈人家讲是龙爪刨腾的痕迹,但是奈何高桥不得。"

Gaoqiao Bridge

Longchuan River, Jietou Town, Tengchong, Yunnan Province, built in 1466 AD.

This timber beam covered bridge has two piers and three spans. It is 35 meters long, 2 meters wide, and 25 meters high. It has the highest piers of all covered bridges in China. Longchuan River has its source in Gaoligong Mountain, and its large volume accumulates upon entering Gaoqiao Gorge. Du Fuguang (born in 1963 in Jietou Town, Zhangjiaying Village), explained that during the rainy seasons, the rapid stream of the Longchuan River dashes against the cliffs of Gaoqiao Gorge, and as a result, the surface of the cliff walls is riddled with abrasions. Old people say this is a sign of a dragon's paw, one though that is helpless when met with the Gaoqiao Bridge.

彩凤桥

云南省云龙县白石镇顺荡村，明崇祯（1628—1644年）

又名大花桥，始建于明崇祯（1628—1644年）年间，是连通兰坪、鹤庆、丽江、剑川要津，也是顺荡五井盐产运往滇西北乃至西藏地区盐马古道的必经节点。木梁单跨伸臂式廊桥，长33.3米、宽4.7米、高11.3米、跨径27米。桥架采用方木交错叠架逐层高拱，使用大木梁合龙。为县级文物保护单位。

Caifeng Bridge

Shundang Village, Baishi Town, Yunlong County, Yunan Province, built during 1628-1644 AD.

It is also called Dahua Bridge. It was constructed sometime between 1628 AD and 1644 AD. It connects Lanping, Heqing, Lijiang and Jianchuan. It also was an essential node on the Ancient Salt and Horse Road for the transportation of salt from Yunnan's historically renowned five salt wells (one of which was located in Shundang Village) to northwest Yunnan and even to Tibet. The covered bridge is a single-span timber cantilever arch beam bridge. It has a total length of 33.3 meters, a width of 4.7 meters, a height of 11.3 meters and a span of 27 meters. The bridge has a high arch formed by stacking staggered square timbers. The arch is closed with the use of large timber beams. It has been listed as a historical and cultural sites protected at the county level.

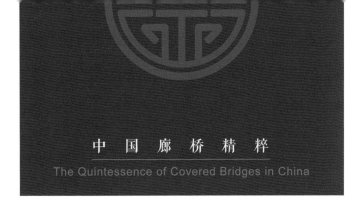

中 国 廊 桥 精 粹

The Quintessence of Covered Bridges in China

清 代

1644—1911 年

　　清代时，廊桥的建造犹如雨后春笋，成为继明代之后又一个快速持续发展时期，并且对近现代廊桥建造影响深远。特别值得一提的是，康熙、乾隆两位皇帝各六次南巡，将江南地区的廊桥文化带到了长城脚下的承德避暑山庄和皇城清漪园（颐和园），使廊桥文化向北延伸了六百公里。这个时期，廊桥建造师世家开始形成，传承至今的有福建省寿宁县郑多金家族、屏南县黄春财家族、屏南县韦学星家族和浙江省泰顺县董直机、曾家快师徒等，他们将工匠精髓薪火相传，延续着中国古代廊桥的血脉。也正是这一时期，木拱廊桥的建造范围越过浙南、闽北地区，在湖南、湖北、云南落地生根，与当地造桥技艺相融合，使木拱廊桥更加丰富多彩。

Qing Dynasty

(1644–1911 AD)

During the Qing Dynasty, the construction of covered bridges flourished like bamboo shoots after a spring rain, marking another period of rapid and sustained development following the Ming Dynasty, with profound influences on the construction of modern covered bridges. Notably, Emperors Kangxi and Qianlong each made six southern tours, bringing the covered bridge culture of the Jiangnan region to the Summer Resort in Chengde and the Qingyi Garden (Summer Palace), extending this culture northward by six hundred kilometers. During this time, families of skilled covered bridge builders began to emerge, including the Zheng Duojin family in Shouning County, Fujian Province, the Huang Chuncai family and the Wei Xuexing family in Pingnan County, and master and apprentice Dong Zhiji and Zeng Jiakuai in Taishun County, Zhejiang Province. These families have passed down the essence of craftsmanship, continuing the lineage of ancient Chinese covered bridges. It was also during this period that the construction of wooden arch covered bridges expanded beyond southern Zhejiang and northern Fujian, taking root in Hunan, Hubei, and Yunnan, where it integrated with local bridge-building techniques, enriching the diversity of wooden arch covered bridges.

水榭廊桥

河北省承德避暑山庄热河湖，清康熙四十八年（1709年）

承德避暑山庄热河湖东侧界墙泄水闸，于清康熙四十八年（1709年）增辟荷花湖时改建为水榭廊桥。由石条桥墩、平梁桥面、木柱木梁、歇山顶凉亭组成。中间大亭五墩六孔，南北小亭各有一侧孔。廊桥两端各有牌坊一座，横匾保存乾隆皇帝题词。南端为"远碧鲸横""晴宵虹亘"，北端为"古嵩碧霞""阆风涤碧"。

Shuixie Covered Bridge

Rehe Lake at the Summer Resort of Chengde, Hebei Province, built in 1709 AD.

There is a floodgate on the east boundary wall of the Rehe Lake at the Summer Resort of Chengde. In 1709 AD, during the expansion of Lotus Lake, the floodgate was rebuilt into a covered bridge. It consists of stone piers, a flat beam deck, timber columns, and timber beams and has a pavilion with a hip-and-gable roof. The big pavilion in the middle of the bridge contains five piers and six spans. Small pavilions on the north and south ends of the bridge each have a span underneath them. Each end of the bridge has a memorial archway, hanging plaques are inscribed with the words of Emperor Qianlong (1736-1795 AD). One on the southern end, reads,"the far moon is crossing the sky" and "making the night sky bright". One on the north end reads "the ancient Song Mountain's depth is magnificent" and "Langfeng Mountain's emits a jasper light".

柳桥

北京市颐和园西堤，清乾隆十五年（1750年）

乾隆皇帝下江南时，见到杭州西湖的玉带桥非常喜欢，即令随行画师绘图，添入自己创意在清漪园（清光绪十四年重建后改名为颐和园）西堤建造四座廊桥，在园内万字河上建造一座廊桥。五座廊桥形态各异，美轮美奂。乾隆皇帝为柳桥赋诗："蓄眼云山影荡摇，玉峰塔矗翠林标。榜人拽使樯竿倒，却为长堤过柳桥。"

Liuqiao Bridge

the Western Embankment, the Summer Palace, Beijing, built in 1750 AD.

During a visit to Hangzhou, Emperor Qianlong was attracted by Yudai Bridge in the West Lake, so he asked painters to draw pictures of this bridge. Then, based on the pictures and his own ideas, the emperor ordered craftsmen to build four covered bridges in the western embankment and one on the Wanzi River of Qingyi Garden (the former name of the Summer Palace after it was reconstructed in 1888 AD). The five covered bridges, of different shapes and structures, are exceedingly harmonious and beautiful. Emperor Qianlong once wrote a poem for the Liuqiao Bridge: "Shadows of clouds and mountains are shaking, and Yufeng Pagoda in the green forest is shining. With a pole in hand, the boatman rowed to the Liuqiao Bridge to see the long dike."

清代 1644—1911年

荇桥

北京市颐和园万字河，清乾隆二十三年（1758 年）

　　清光绪十八年（1892 年）按原样修缮。东西走向，长 25 米、宽 4.8 米、高 6.5 米，两侧各有 25 级台阶。黄色花岗石砌筑桥洞三孔，中孔可过小船。主桥孔两侧设立棱柱金刚船首，上端斗拱表面站立镇水瑞兽两只。荇桥从设计选材到施工装饰一丝不苟，美轮美奂，无可挑剔。

Xingqiao Bridge

Wanzi River, the Summer Palace, Beijing, built in 1758 AD.

In 1892 AD, the bridge was rebuilt according to its original form. Running from east to west, this bridge is 25 meters long, 4.8 meters wide, and 6.5 meters high, with 25 steps on each side. The three bridge spans are built of yellow granite, and the middle one is high enough to allow boats to pass through. The columns on either side of the span incorporate "diamond" bases built in the form of the bows of a ship. On the columns' *dougong* bracket tops are figures of two auspicious beasts thought to protect the bridge from the flood. Built with meticulous design and decorations, the bridge is indeed very impressive and perfect.

豳风桥

北京市颐和园西堤，清乾隆（1736—1795年）

豳风桥是一座长方形的廊桥，乾隆皇帝命名为桑苎（泛指农桑种植事业）桥。清咸丰十年（1860年），桑苎桥被英法联军烧毁。清光绪十四年（1888年）修整后改名为豳风桥。

Binfeng Bridge

the Western Embankment, the Summer Palace, Beijing, built during 1736-1795 AD.

The Binfeng Bridge is a rectangular covered bridge. Emperor Qianlong named it the Mulberry Bridge (Sangzhu Bridge, in reference to the cultivation of mulberry trees, an important part of the sericulture silk farming industry). In 1860 AD, Sangzhu Bridge was burned down by the Anglo-French Allied Forces. It was rebuilt in 1888 AD and was renamed Binfeng Bridge.

康庄桥

甘肃省文县铁楼藏族乡白马河,清光绪(1875—1908年)

白马河畔铁楼藏族乡是白马人居住地。乡民说,冬季大雪封山,会有大熊猫沿着山路过廊桥到村子里觅食,每家都会拿出最好的东西让大熊猫吃饱。全木结构平梁廊桥,长20米、宽4米、高4米,五开间,顶覆小青瓦,两端建有矮泥墙凉亭式门楼。

Kangzhuang Bridge

Baima River, Tielou Tibetan Autonomous Township, Wenxian County, Gansu Province, built during 1875-1908 AD.

Tielou Tibetan Autonomous Township is where Baima people live. Villagers say that when snow seals the mountain pass in winter, pandas will walk along the mountain road to find food in villages, and whoever lives in a house that the pandas arrive at will always give them their best food until the pandas are full. The Kangzhuang Bridge is a timber beam bridge. The bridge's gallery house has 5 bays. The bridge is 20 meters long, 4 meters wide, and 4 meters high. It is covered on top with small grey tiles. On either end, it has pavilion-style gatehouse built with low rammed-earth walls.

东河桥

陕西省紫阳县高桥镇,清乾隆六十年(1795年)

《紫阳县志》载:"高桥在县南内权河,一跨西河,一跨东河,清乾隆末杨道仁建。清嘉庆九年(1804年)周桂重建。清道光三年(1823年)周泰兴倡建石桥,清道光七年(1827年)庞泰然捐修西河桥。清道光十二年(1832年)周一刚捐修东河桥,清光绪乙己年(1905年)武生金玉堂,左伦忠募资补修。"为全木结构平梁式廊桥,跨径15米、自高3米、宽3米。为省级文物保护单位。

Donghe Bridge

Gaoqiao Town, Ziyang County, Shaanxi Province, built in 1795 AD.

According to the *Ziyang County Annals*, there were Gaoqiao Bridges that spanned over the Neiquan River in the southern part of the county, with one bridge crossing the Neiquan River's west river and another spanning its east river. The bridges were built in the late 18th Century by Yang Daoren and reconstructed in 1804 AD by Zhou Gui. Later in 1823 AD Zhou Taixing proposed building a stone bridge. In 1827 AD Pang Tairan funded the Xihe Bridge's restoration. The Donghe Bridge was then renovated by Zhou Yigang in 1832 AD. In 1905 AD, the Donghe Bridge was overhauled with funding from Jin Yutang and Zuo Lunzhong. It is a flat beam timber covered bridge. Its span is 15 meters, and it is 3 meters high and 3 meters wide. It has been listed as a historical and cultural sites protected at the provincial level.

西河桥

陕西省紫阳县高桥镇,清乾隆六十年(1795年)

西河桥距东河桥150米,采用同样的结构、尺寸和建造形式。木平梁廊桥长15米、宽3米、高3米。古镇享有盛名,原因即是遗存陕西全省仅有的2座双梁木平清代廊桥。修缮总监、帮办、经理、首仕、木匠及捐修人士的姓名,铭刻于桥顶横梁。尽管被列为省级文物保护单位,廊桥依然是古镇河边居民日常通道。

Xihe Bridge

Gaoqiao Town, Ziyang County, Shaanxi Province, built in 1795 AD.

Located 150 meters from the Donghe Bridge, the Xihe Bridge has almost the same structure, size, and construction. It also is a flat beam timber covered bridge. It is 15 meters long, 3 meters wide and 3 meters high. This ancient town enjoys great fame for possessing the only two double set of covered bridges built in the Qing Dynasty in Shaanxi Province. Names of the bridge's directors of renovations, assistants, managers, chief officials, carpenters, and donors are engraved on the bridge's top beams. Although the bridge has been listed as a historical and cultural sites protected at the provincial level, it still functions as a means for passage for the residents living by the ancient town's river.

万寿桥

重庆市石柱土家族自治县三河镇拱桥村，清乾隆四十一年（1776年）

石拱木屋廊桥，东西走向，横跨龙沙河，巍然挺立，长18米、宽4米、高15米、跨径7.8米。廊桥两侧各有一座叠石"天梯"，东面石阶29层，西面石阶28层，为中国石阶最多的石拱廊桥。

Wanshou Bridge

Gongqiao Village, Sanhe Town, Shizhu Tujia Autonomous County, Chongqing, built in 1776 AD.

Wanshou Bridge is a stone arch wooden bridge, runs east to west, spanning the Longsha River. It stands majestically, measuring 18 meters in length, 4 meters in width, and 15 meters in height, with a span of 7.8 meters. On both sides of the covered bridge, there are stone "heavenly ladders"; the eastern side features 29 stone steps, while the western side has 28 steps. This bridge is recognized as the covered stone arch bridge with the most stone steps in China.

锡福桥

重庆市丰都县，清乾隆五十七年（1792年）

又名赐福桥、石佛桥，独孔木廊结构，古时候方圆几十里百姓出行就依靠这座桥。以前没有大桥，雨季常有行人过河落水与溺亡事故发生。当地乡绅倡导捐资、集资，请风水师勘察地形、确定桥址，召集工匠建成。竣工典礼上，路过的新媳妇孙蒋氏雯秀在桥心高喊一声"新人踩新桥，踩不断的铁板桥"。从此"媳妇桥"（为锡福桥谐音）叫响开来。《丰都县志》记，"新石桥建成后，一新媳脱簪珥足之，故名媳妇桥"。

Xifu Bridge

Fengdu County, Chongqing, built in 1792 AD.

Also called Cifu Bridge or Shifo Bridge, it is a single-span timber structure. In old times, it was an indispensable passageway for people from tens of miles all around who relied on it for traveling back and forth. Before its construction, there were often travelers who drowned in the river when trying to cross during the rainy season. As a result, the local gentry raised funds for a bridge's construction, invited *fengshui* masters to investigate the land and determine the location for the bridge and convened craftsmen to build it. In a ceremony during its completion, the bride, named Wenxiu, walked on the bridge, stood in the middle and called out, "The bride and groom tread on the new bridge, over its iron boards that will not be broken." Since then, the name of the bridge has also been Xifu Bridge (*xifu*, meaning daughter-in-law, is used to refer to one's wife in Chinese, also a homophone of Xifu Bridge). As it is recorded in *the History of Fengdu County*, "When the new stone bridge was established, a bride walked on it without wearing her hairpin and earrings, hence its name is the Xifu Bridge."

回龙桥

重庆市酉阳土家族苗族自治县清泉乡龙溪河口，清同治十年（1871年）

单孔八字支撑穿斗式全木结构木拱廊桥，长29米、宽4.3米、高5米，十开间，距水面（非洪水期）40米。龙溪河口是风大水猛的险地，匠师在坚固的基台上以十数根粗大杉木做八字支撑，再用圆木横梁衔接支撑点，上铺木板桥面建廊屋，两端砖石垒砌拱门。各种规格材料铆扣衔固，未用铁钉铁箍，具备很强的抗风抗洪能力。2010年，乌江洪水倒灌龙溪河，回龙桥在水中浸泡一个多月未受伤损。

Huilong Bridge

over the mouth of Longxi River, Qingquan Township, Youyang Tujia and Miao Autonomous County, Chongqing, built in 1871 AD.

Huilong Bridge is a single span timber arch bridge with *bazi*-shaped supports and a *chuandou* style gallery house. It is built entirely of wood. Its gallery house consists of 10 bays, and the bridge is 29 meters long, 4.3 meters wide and 5 meters high. The river runs 40 meters below the bridge during the non-flood period. The mouth of Longxi River is dangerous because of the high winds and swift current there. As a result, the master carpenters placed dozens of thick timbers of China fir on top of the rigid foundation to form the *bazi*-shaped supporting members. Then they used log crossbeams to link together the nodes of the supporting members. Timber boards were laid on top of the deck, and a gallery house was built on top with archways composed of stone masonry at either end. All of the bridge's connections are constructed without the use of a single iron nail or clamp, and it is extremely wind and flood resistant. Huilong Bridge was immersed in the flood from Wujiang River for more than a month in 2010, and even then was not damaged.

两河风雨桥

重庆市忠县白石镇两河社区，清嘉庆（1796—1820 年）

早期河道架有几条石板，供乡民往来，清嘉庆（1796—1820 年）年间修建石拱桥。1912 年，乡民集资在石拱桥面上加盖桥廊，从此成为四里八乡赶圩集市。桥长 37.7 米、宽 5 米、高 8.5 米，两墩三孔，跨径均为 9 米。桥身使用当地山石砌就，是忠县最高、跨径最大的古桥。2017 年 11 月，政府出资维修桥廊。为县级文物保护单位。

Lianghe Fengyu Bridge

Lianghe Community, Baishi Town, Zhongxian County, Chongqing, built during 1796-1820 AD.

This bridge originally consisted of a few stone slabs that allowed villagers to travel back and forth. During 1796-1820 AD, it was built as a stone arch bridge. In 1912 AD, villagers raised funds to build a gallery house on top of the stone bridge to serve as a market place for nearby residents, and since then it has served as the site for market fairs for people in the surrounding villages. The three-span bridge is 37.7 meters long, 5 meters wide and 8.5 meters high. Each span is 9 meters long. It was built with rocks from the local mountains. It is the highest covered bridge with the longest span in Zhongxian County and was renovated by the government in November 2017. It has been listed as a historical and cultural sites protected at the county level.

马家滩桥

重庆市开州区紫水乡紫水村,清代(1644—1911年)

纯木结构平梁廊桥,凌驾于紫水河谷险要峡口。长约10米、宽1.6米,距水面高10余米,三开间,是村民下田春播秋收、上山砍柴采药的重要通道。

Majiatan Bridge

Zishui Village, Zishui Township, Kaizhou District, Chongqing, built during 1644-1911 AD.

Majiatan Bridge is a purely wooden flat-beam covered bridge, situated above the treacherous gorge of the Zishui River Valley. It is approximately 10 meters in length and 1.6 meters in width, with an elevation of over 10 meters above the water surface. Its gallery house has 3 bays. It serves as an important passage for villagers engaged in spring planting, autumn harvesting, and collecting firewood and medicinal herbs in the mountains.

五星桥

重庆市合川区双槐镇双门村与四川省华蓥市庆华镇三河村流溪河，清道光二年（1822年）

一座廊桥跨越一省一市，在中国绝无仅有。五星桥以中线为界，桥南为重庆市，桥北为四川省。桥两岸几十户村民在农历初一、十五会餐，主食是稻米饭，主菜是豆花，配上辣椒酱，真是香喷喷的。桥上原有6户人家，四川省、重庆市各3家，2012年为恢复廊道，由文物部门劝离。五星桥又名火烧滩桥，长60米、宽6米、高5米，四墩五孔，每孔跨径8.8米，桥廊为穿斗式结构硬山顶。五星桥被列为四川省、重庆市文物保护单位。

Wuxing Bridge

over Liuxi River at Sanhe Village, Qinghua Town, Huaying, Sichuan Province and also in Shuangmen Village, Shuanghuai Town, Hechuan District, Chongqing, built in 1822 AD.

It is the only bridge lying at the boundary between Sichuan and Chongqing. The boundary between the two areas lies in the middle of the bridge, with Chongqing's territory covering the south of the bridge and Sichuan's the north. Villagers from the dozens of families on each side of the bridge dine together on the first and fifteenth days of every lunar month on the bridge. The main dishes are rice, tofu pudding, and chilli sauce, which smell delicious. Three families from Sichuan and three from Chongqing lived on the bridge until 2012, when the cultural heritage department moved them away to restore the bridge's covered road. The bridge, also named Huoshaotan Bridge, is a *chuandou* style structure with a flush gable roof. The five-span covered bridge with a stone arch is 60 meters long, 6 meters wide and 5 meters high. Each of its spans is 8.8 meters long. Wuxing Bridge has been listed as a historical and cultural sites protected by both Sichuan and Chongqing.

烟雨廊桥

四川省汉源县河南乡，清代（1644—1911 年）

贯木平梁全木结构廊桥，长 14 米、宽 3 米，五开间，单檐悬山顶，桥口设置挑阁。烟雨廊桥原名八里铺廊桥，连通灵关古道。为市级文物保护单位。

Yanyu Covered Bridge

Henan Township, Hanyuan County, Sichuan Province, built during 1644-1911 AD.

Yanyu Covered Bridge is a fully wooden flat-beam structure, measuring 14 meters in length and 3 meters in width. Its gallery house has 5 bays, and has a single-eaved hip roof. It features a cantilevered pavilion at the entrance. Originally named Balipu Covered Bridge, connecting to the Lingguan Ancient Road. It has been listed as a historical and cultural sites protected at the municipal level.

接龙桥

四川省南江县公山镇卫星村，清代（1644—1911年）

接龙桥自古连通米仓古道东榆铺段南江河东段。石墩木梁廊桥，长 39 米、宽 5.5 米，桥顶距河床高 10 米。取用米仓古道皇柏林中的皇柏制作的梁材，长 17 米、宽厚均为 0.4 米。廊屋为穿斗式结构，顶覆小青瓦。为省级文物保护单位。

Jielong Bridge

Weixing Village, Gongshan Town, Nanjiang County, Sichuan Province, built during 1644-1911 AD.

Jielong Bridge has historically connected the Dongyupu section of the Micang Ancient Road and the eastern section of the Nanjiang River. It is a wooden beam covered bridge supported by stone piers, measuring 39 meters in length and 5.5 meters in width, with a height of 10 meters above the riverbed. The beams, sourced from the cypress trees in the Huangbai forest along the Micang Ancient Road, each measure 17 meters in length and 0.4 meters in both width and thickness. Its gallery house is a *chuandou* style structure and covered with small grey tiles on the roof. It has been listed as a historical and cultural sites at the provincial level.

三曲桥

四川省崇州市罨画池博物馆，清代（1644—1911年）

罨画池始建于唐代（618—907年），初为蜀州（崇州）州署郡圃（待客园林）兼作驿站，后代屡有扩建，为全国重点文物保护单位。三曲桥为两座立柱式石墩三孔木构廊桥，中廊高，两端低，整座桥不在一条直线上，故得此名。其状犹如彩虹，因而又名为"飞虹桥"。三曲桥是外池和内池的界桥，北池宽阔，南池精巧，与周边环境相得益彰，通透美观，游人多有夸赞。

Sanqu Bridge

Yanhua Pond Museum, Chongzhou, Sichuan Province, built during 1644-1911 AD.

Yanhua Pond was originally established during the Tang Dynasty (618-907 AD) as a guest garden and relay station for the Shuzhou (Chongzhou) prefectural government. It has undergone several expansions in subsequent generations and has been listed as a major historical and cultural sites protected at the national level. Sanqu Bridge is a wooden covered bridge supported by two column-style stone piers with three spans. The central corridor is elevated, while both ends are lower, resulting in a non-linear design, which gives the bridge its name. Its shape resembles a rainbow, thus it is also known as Feihong Bridge (Flying Rainbow Bridge). Sanqu Bridge serves as the boundary between the outer pond and the inner pond. The northern pond is wide, while the southern pond is intricately designed, complementing the surrounding environment with its transparency and aesthetic appeal, earning much praise from visitors.

弥江桥

四川省盐亭县莲花湖乡弥江村，清康熙五十三年（1714年）

两墩三孔木屋廊桥，因弥江寺在侧得名。跨弥江河，东西走向，长12米、宽2.2米，三根大圆木为梁，上铺木板，桥中部架单檐悬山顶楼阁，设木梯，两端桥屋均为单檐桥头，建门坊、装饰斗拱。桥头有清乾隆五十四年（1789年）补葺纪事桥碑。为市级文物保护单位。

Mijiang Bridge

Mijiang Village, Lianhuahu Township, Yanting County, Sichuan Province, built in 1714 AD.

Mijiang Bridge is a wooden covered bridge supported by two piers and featuring three spans, named after the nearby Mijiang Temple. Spanning the Mijiang River, the bridge runs east to west and measures 12 meters in length and 2.2 meters in width. It is constructed with three large round timbers as beams, topped with wooden planks. The central section features a single-eaved hip-roof pavilion with a wooden ladder, while both ends of the bridge house single-eaved pavilions with decorative archways. A stele documenting repairs made in 1789 AD is located at the bridgehead. It has been listed as a historical and cultural sites protected at the municipal level.

合益桥

四川省江油市二郎庙镇，清乾隆（1736—1795年）

合益桥位于江油市二郎庙镇新街、老街分界小河，原是"飞檐列栏、丹腹浩瀚"通车马的木制廊桥。清嘉庆五年（1800年）春，山匪抢劫未得手，恼怒之下将合益桥烧毁。清嘉庆十四年（1809年）乡民募资集材，招募工匠民工建成两墩三孔的石拱廊桥。长24米、高8米、宽6米。清道光二十年（1840年）多方资助修缮。

Heyi Bridge

Erlangmiao Town, Jiangyou, Sichuan Province, built during 1736-1795 AD.

Heyi Bridge crosses a river which serves as the boundary between the new street and the old street of Erlangmiao Town in Jiangyou. It was originally a grand timber covered bridge with upturned eaves and railings over which carriages passed. In the spring of 1800 AD, bandits attempted to rob but failed, so they burned the bridge down in anger. In 1809 AD, villagers raised funds and recruited craftsmen to rebuild the bridge as a three span two pier stone arch covered bridge. The bridge is 24 meters long, 8 meters high, and 6 meters wide. The bridge was repaired again in 1840 AD, funded by contributions from many parties.

姊妹桥

四川省绵阳市安州区桑枣镇，清同治十一年（1872年）

清同治十一年（1872年），乡民公议出钱出力建成全木结构木平廊桥。又名双木桥、高桥、五福桥。两座廊桥高矮形制一致、宽窄长短相同，相隔6米，故称姊妹桥。河心岩石为桥墩，自成两孔，长11米、宽4米、高3.5米，加墩台连阶总长29米。主梁由10根直径40厘米圆木并聚而成，桥面铺设厚木板，坚固耐用。穿斗式结构各组构件扣榫工艺不见一钉一铆，单脊挑檐悬山顶，桥头建有牌楼。

Zimei Bridges

Sangzao Town, Anzhou District, Mianyang, Sichuan Province, built in 1872 AD.

Also known as Shuangmu Bridge, Gaoqiao Bridge, and Wufu Bridge, the two bridges were built in 1872 AD with funds collected by the local villagers. They have the same shape and are separated by 6 meters. Because of this, they are called Zimei Bridges. A rock outcropping in the middle of the river serves as a shared natural bridge pier for both of the bridges, hence creating two spans. The bridges are 11 meters in length, 4 meters in width, 3.5 meters in height and when including the rock pier in the center of the bridges, the combined length of them is 29 meters. For each bridge, the main beam member is composed by combining together ten logs that are 40 centimeters thick. The bridge's deck is covered with solid and thick timber boards. Every component of the *chuandou* style construction is completed using mortise and tenon technology so that not a single nail can be found in the joints. The bridges' gallery houses are topped with single-ridge roofs with upturned eaves.

波日桥

四川省新龙县雅砻江,清代(1644—1911年)

波日桥由藏族建造师设计并指挥构筑。叠木伸臂式拱梁廊桥,长125米、宽3米、跨径60米。有"康巴第一桥"盛誉,被列为全国重点文物保护单位。1930年,西藏噶厦政府军队进驻新龙,烧毁6座藏式伸臂桥,唯有波日桥幸存。1933年,由民间建筑师率领藏族工匠维修一新。

Bori Bridge

Yalong River, Xinlong County, Sichuan Province, built during 1644-1911 AD.

Bori Bridge was designed and constructed under the guidance of a Tibetan architect. It is a timber cantilever arch-beam bridge composed of combined wooden beams. It is 125 meters long, 3 meters wide, and has a span of 60 meters. It is called "The Kham Area's Greatest Bridge" and is listed as a major historical and cultural sites protected at the national level. In 1930 AD, the army of the Tibetan Kashag Government Council stationed in Xinlong, burned down six Tibetan-style cantilever bridges. Only the Bori Bridge survived. In 1933 AD, a folk architect, led Tibetan craftsmen in restoring the bridge.

虎啸桥

四川省乐山市峨眉山伏虎寺山腰，清代（1644—1911 年）

　　虎啸桥长 9.9 米、宽 3.3 米、高 8.6 米，为独孔石拱全木结构穿斗式廊桥。两侧设置木栏。廊桥两端建四角飞檐小阁，顶部铺满小青瓦。

Huxiao Bridge

Mountainside of Fuhu Temple, Emei Mountain, Leshan, Sichuan Province, built during 1644-1911 AD.

This is a stone arch timber frame covered bridge with a single span. It is 9.9 meters long, 3.3 meters wide, and 8.6 meters high. The bridge's gallery house is a *chuandou* style structure with timber railing on both sides. Small pavilions stand either side of the bridge, topped with upturned eaves on all four corners and covered with small grey tiles.

龙华凉桥

四川省屏山县龙华镇龙溪，清光绪（1875—1908 年）

　　龙华镇宋代（960—1279 年）始建，为国家级历史文化名镇。发源于大凉山的龙溪穿镇而过，凉桥跨龙溪建造，四墩五孔、木柱木梁、石平瓦顶廊桥。桥墩为石墙形制，上游墩首迎浪石柱上各蹲一只石狮。《龙华凉桥志》记："原名清虹桥，建于清代光绪年间。廊桥式样奇巧美观，为龙华古镇标志性建筑。逢年过节、赶场办事，镇上的人都要集聚在凉桥之畔，平常堪为古镇人众纳凉休闲之胜地。1964 年、1974 年修缮。"

Longhua Liangqiao Bridge

Longxi Creek, Longhua Town, Pingshan County, Sichuan Province, built during 1875-1908 AD.

Longhua Town was built in the Song Dynasty (960-1279 AD) and is the national famous historical and cultural town in China. The Longxi Creek, which originates in the Daliang Mountain, passes through the town, and the bridge spans it. It is a covered bridge with four piers and five spans, with timber columns, timber beams and a roof covered with flat stone tiles. The piers are in the shape of stone walls with lions squatting on top, greeting the oncoming waters. The *Chronicles of Longhua Liangqiao Bridge* records that "Formerly known as Qinghong Bridge, the bridge was built during 1875-1908 AD. The style of the covered bridge is interesting and appealing. It is the most famous architectural landmark in the Longhua Ancient Town. During the Lunar New Year, or when going to the fair, people in the town gather besides the bridge, which is a famous scenic site and a place for the locals to enjoy and to cool down by. It was repaired in 1964 and 1974."

保兴桥

云南省西畴县兴街镇畴阳河，清乾隆十三年（1748年）

横跨畴阳河（牛羊河），自古是滇东南地区与安南国（越南）商品贸易、走亲访友、物资交流的通道。又名牛羊太平桥。始建于清乾隆十三年（1748年），多次大修。桥全长27米、宽3.2米、高5米，桥廊进深九间。桥的两边设置长板椅，供路人避雨纳凉。桥的两端建有桥楼，桥楼石砌八字形防水墙，内侧立石碑五块。中孔上端建砖木结构双层风雨亭，重檐翘角悬山顶覆黄色琉璃瓦。两侧有1米高石栏，两端各有一对迎门石狮。

Baoxing Bridge

Chouyang River, Xingjie Town, Xichou County, Yunnan Province, built in 1748 AD.

Spanning the Chouyang River (also known as the Niuyang River), since ancient times the bridge has been a conduit for commercial and material trade—and for the travel of guests and relatives—between southeast Yunnan Province and Vietnam. It is also called Niuyang Taiping Bridge. First built in 1748 AD, it has since undergone many major repairs. The bridge is 27 meters long, 3.2 meters wide, and 5 meters high and the gallery house on top is 9 bays long. There are benches on both sides of the bridge for people to use to take shelter from rain or to enjoy the cool temperature in the bridge. At both ends of the bridge, there are bridge houses with stone *bazi*-shaped walls that provide protection from the rain. There are five stone stele inside the bridge houses as well. A brick and timber pavilion for shelter from the wind and rain stands in the middle span of the bridge. It has two stories and is topped with a hip and gable roof with upturned eaves, covered with yellow glazed tiles. Each side of the bridge has a 1 meter high stone railing, and a pair of stone welcoming lions greet visitors at either end.

清代 1644—1911年

永镇桥

云南省云龙县长新乡大达河，清乾隆六年（1741年）

建于清乾隆六年（1741年），清光绪元年（1875年）重修。1985年毁于山洪，1987年复修。长26米、宽4.8米、跨径16米。桥堍上部土砖砌筑凉亭门楼，桥口竖立粗大半圆顶方柱，外侧设挡雨板，内侧安放木凳。凉亭上设卷棚顶，门楼对角悬山顶覆花青瓦。永镇桥属伸臂式木拱廊桥，云龙县、腾冲市各遗存三座。与浙江、福建木拱廊桥的区别是两侧各加装一组梯形方梁作为辅助支撑。

Yongzhen Bridge

Dada River, Changxin Township, Yunlong County, Yunnan Province, built in 1741 AD.

The bridge was constructed in 1741 AD, rebuilt in 1875 AD and restored in 1987 after being destroyed by a mountain flood in 1985. The bridge is 26 meters long, 4.8 meters wide, and has a span of 16 meters. Above its abutments are pavilion archways formed from adobe bricks. At the entrance, there is a large semi-circular column. Skirts run alongside the perimeter to protect the bridge from rain, and wooden benches are placed inside. The *juanpengding* (round ridge roofs) cover the pavilion, and the slopes of the gables on the gate building are topped with different types of grey tiles. Yongzhen Bridge is a timber cantilever arch covered bridge. Similar covered bridges can be found in Yunlong and Tengchong. These bridges install a trapezoidal assemblage of beams on each side to serve as auxiliary supports, making them unlike the timber arch beams in Zhejiang and Fujian.

通京桥

云南省云龙县长新乡包罗村,清乾隆四十一年（1776年）

曾名通金桥，因附近"白羊厂"出产的白银运往北京，取"财通京城"之意。清乾隆四十九年（1784年）、清道光十九年（1839年）、1962年维修。1993年8月29日被百年不遇山洪冲毁，1994年6月依照古貌修复。独孔全木结构伸臂式廊桥，大小构件采用木桁扣榫连接。与浙南、闽北木拱廊桥有差别，但同属木拱廊桥。

Tongjing Bridge

Baoluo Village, Changxin Township, Yunlong County, Yunnan Province, built in 1776 AD.

The bridge was originally known as Tongjin Bridge. Later, since the silver ore from the Baiyang Mine was transported from here to the capital Beijing, the bridge was renamed Tongjing Bridge (in Chinese, *tong* means transport, and *jing* means capital, which then, as now, was Beijing). Three major repairs on the bridge were conducted in 1784 AD, 1839 AD, and 1962. On August 29, 1993, the bridge was damaged by a one-in-a-hundred-year flood, and in June 1994, it was rebuilt in accordance with its old look. It is a single-span timber cantilever covered bridge. Both its large and small components are connected through the use of timber crosspieces and mortise and tenon joins. It is different from the timber arch bridges in southern Zhejiang Province and northern Fujian Province, but it still can be considered to be a timber arch bridge.

天缘桥

云南省建水县泸江河，清雍正六年（1728年）

清嘉庆四年（1799年）重修，三孔石拱亭桥，长121米、宽8米，主桥跨河43米，南引桥长36米、北引桥长42米，桥孔相隔8米。船首形桥墩中孔高10米，侧孔高9米，南北引桥向东西方向延伸呈S形。双层重檐、四方八角、飞檐攒尖顶，亭阁高大雄伟。桥头石壁遗存一方清雍正八年（1730年）残碑，依稀可见"游览斯桥者，只宜安静观望，不得擅毁神像、阁亭砖瓦、墙壁、狮象等类。倘刁恶不羁，扭送官究决不宽贷"等文字。为省级文物保护单位。

Tianyuan Bridge

Lujiang River, Jianshui County, built in 1728 AD.

The bridge was rebuilt in 1799 AD. The stone arch pavilion bridge has three spans and is 121 meters long and 8 meters wide. The main bridge is 43 meters long, the southern approach to it is 36 meters long, and the northern approach to it is 42 meters long, with a distance of 8 meters between the spans. The pier in the middle span is formed in the shape of a ship's bow and is 10 meters tall. The adjacent piers are 9 meters tall. The north and south approaches extend first in an east and west direction respectively, forming an overall S-shaped bridge. The two-story pavilion building in the center of the bridge has two sets of eaves, the bottom set with four sides and the upper with eight edges and a pyramidal top. It is a tall and magnificent structure. The remnant of a stele, erected in 1730 AD, is installed at the front of the bridge. It reads: "Visitors of the bridge should peacefully view it and must not destroy its statues, pavilion tiles, walls, lion statues, and other objects. If one acts hatefully and unruly, they will be seized and delivered to the officials for judgement without mercy..." The bridge has been listed as a historical and cultural sites protected at the provincial level.

乡会桥

云南省建水县西庄镇新房村泸江河,清嘉庆十九年（1814年）

砖石结构两墩三孔石拱廊桥,主桥长18米,引桥长25米,宽7米,高6米。两层廊屋中的下层为通道,上层为魁星阁。

Xianghui Bridge

Lujiang River, Xinfang Village, Xizhuang Town, Jianshui County, Yunnan Province, built in 1814 AD.

This is a masonry covered bridge with two piers and three stone arch spans. The main bridge structure is 18 meters long; the bridge approach is 25 meters long, it is 7 meters wide and 6 meters high. The first story of the two-story gallery house serves as a corridor for travel, and the second floor is a pavilion for *kuixing* (the Taoist god of examinations).

永顺桥

湖北省利川市毛坝镇三湾河峡谷,清嘉庆十二年（1807年）

　　永顺桥建在三湾河峡谷最窄处。由乡绅周正已、张启荣发起修建。独孔木拱伸臂平梁式全木结构廊桥，不用一钉一铆，以杉木凿榫衔接。长32.5米、宽3米、高40米。桥基依托坚固石壁，三排（组）圆木双方向斜伸支撑双排圆木横梁作为主体桥架，上部廊柱与桥架贯通形成坚固整体，再以两侧木栏加固。永顺桥被列为市级文物保护单位，于清光绪六年（1880年）、1952年、1967年、1991年修缮。

Yongshun Bridge

Sanwanhe Canyon, Maoba Town, Lichuan, Hubei Province, built in 1807 AD.

Yongshun Bridge was built at the narrowest part of the Sanwanhe Canyon. Local gentry Zhou Zhengyi and Zhang Qirong called for the bridge's construction. It is a single span timber cantilever arch-beam covered bridge. Utilizing mortise-tenon technology, it doesn't use a single nail or rivet; instead, tenons are chiseled out of China fir wood to connect the structure together. It is 32.5 meters long, 3 meters wide, and 40 meters high. Its foundation is formed from a solid stone wall. Three rows (assemblages) of logs extend diagonally in either direction to support two rows of crossbeams, forming the main bridge structure. The columns in the gallery house in the upper bridge structure pass through the main bridge structure, forming a solid overall unit, which is strengthened through the use of timber railings on either side of the bridge. It has been listed as a historical and cultural sites protected at the municipal level. The bridge has been repaired in 1880 AD, 1952, 1967, and 1991.

深溪河桥

湖北省来凤县革勒车镇白果村，清同治二年（1863年）

深溪河桥藏于山林田野深处，发现十分不易。深溪河桥由张姓乡绅倡捐修建。一墩两孔凉亭式廊桥，长25米、宽8米、高6.8米。1963年、1979年被山洪冲毁，于1964年、1981年修复。1981年修复时将桥墩升高1米，提高了抗洪能力。

Shenxihe Bridge

Baiguo Village, Geleche Town, Laifeng County, Hubei Province, built in 1863 AD.

Shenxihe Bridge is hidden deep in the woods and fields, and it is quite difficult to get there. Shenxihe Bridge was built at the initiative of a member of the local gentry surnamed Zhang, who called for contributions for the effort. The "cool pavilion" covered bridge has one pier and two spans. It is 25 meters long, 8 meters wide, and 6.8 meters high. In 1963 and 1979, it was destroyed by mountain floods and restored in 1964 and 1981. During an overhaul in 1981, the pier was raised by 1 meter to enhance the ability to resist flooding.

龙家桥

湖北省来凤县旧司镇龙桥村打车河峡谷，清光绪四年（1878年）

又名楼房坝桥。一墩两孔全木结构平梁式廊桥，长28.5米、宽2.65米、高7.7米、跨径12.5米，九开间。龙家桥由楼房坝苗族首领龙通成主持，乡民捐资建成。而后每逢清明节雨季来临前，家族首领会召集族人讨论廊桥维护。1979年8月1日深夜，桥廊被特大洪水冲毁，百姓捐款捐粮于次年复建。为省级文物保护单位。

Longjia Bridge

Dachehe Canyon, Longqiao Village, Jiusi Town, Laifeng County, Hubei Province, built in 1878 AD.

Also known as Loufangba Bridge, it is a timber beam bridge with one pier and two spans. It is 28.5 meters long, 2.65 meters wide, 7.7 meters high, and has a span of 12.5 meters. Its gallery house has 9 bays. Long Tongcheng, the head representative of the village's Miao community, is in charge of the bridge. In addition, villagers contribute money to its maintenance. Before the rainy season around the time of the Qingming Festival (which occurs early April), the head will call on the clan to come together to discuss the maintenance of the covered bridge. On August 1, 1979, the bridge's gallery house was destroyed by a huge flood, and in the following year the common people of the village donated money and grain to support its rebuilding. It has been listed as a historical and cultural sites protected at the provincial level.

永福桥

湖南省通道侗族自治县坪坦乡高步村，清乾隆五十年（1785年）

永福桥圆木平梁全木结构，不用一钉一铁，构件卯榫嵌合。独孔叠木平梁、穿斗式木构架，长39米、宽3.8米，跨径16.2米，十一开间。东端建高大望楼，整桥为龙形。清嘉庆十年（1805年）、清道光十五年（1835年）、清同治三年（1864年）、清光绪二十年（1894年）、1936年复建。属于坪坦风雨桥，为全国重点文物保护单位。

深溪河桥

湖北省来凤县革勒车镇白果村，清同治二年（1863年）

深溪河桥藏于山林田野深处，发现十分不易。深溪河桥由张姓乡绅倡捐修建。一墩两孔凉亭式廊桥，长25米、宽8米、高6.8米。1963年、1979年被山洪冲毁，于1964年、1981年修复。1981年修复时将桥墩升高1米，提高了抗洪能力。

Shenxihe Bridge

Baiguo Village, Geleche Town, Laifeng County, Hubei Province, built in 1863 AD.

Shenxihe Bridge is hidden deep in the woods and fields, and it is quite difficult to get there. Shenxihe Bridge was built at the initiative of a member of the local gentry surnamed Zhang, who called for contributions for the effort. The "cool pavilion" covered bridge has one pier and two spans. It is 25 meters long, 8 meters wide, and 6.8 meters high. In 1963 and 1979, it was destroyed by mountain floods and restored in 1964 and 1981. During an overhaul in 1981, the pier was raised by 1 meter to enhance the ability to resist flooding.

龙家桥

湖北省来凤县旧司镇龙桥村打车河峡谷，清光绪四年（1878年）

又名楼房坝桥。一墩两孔全木结构平梁式廊桥，长28.5米、宽2.65米、高7.7米、跨径12.5米，九开间。龙家桥由楼房坝苗族首领龙通成主持，乡民捐资建成。而后每逢清明节雨季来临前，家族首领会召集族人讨论廊桥维护。1979年8月1日深夜，桥廊被特大洪水冲毁，百姓捐款捐粮于次年复建。为省级文物保护单位。

Longjia Bridge

Dachehe Canyon, Longqiao Village, Jiusi Town, Laifeng County, Hubei Province, built in 1878 AD.

Also known as Loufangba Bridge, it is a timber beam bridge with one pier and two spans. It is 28.5 meters long, 2.65 meters wide, 7.7 meters high, and has a span of 12.5 meters. Its gallery house has 9 bays. Long Tongcheng, the head representative of the village's Miao community, is in charge of the bridge. In addition, villagers contribute money to its maintenance. Before the rainy season around the time of the Qingming Festival (which occurs early April), the head will call on the clan to come together to discuss the maintenance of the covered bridge. On August 1, 1979, the bridge's gallery house was destroyed by a huge flood, and in the following year the common people of the village donated money and grain to support its rebuilding. It has been listed as a historical and cultural sites protected at the provincial level.

永福桥

湖南省通道侗族自治县坪坦乡高步村，清乾隆五十年（1785年）

永福桥圆木平梁全木结构，不用一钉一铁，构件卯榫嵌合。独孔叠木平梁、穿斗式木构架，长39米、宽3.8米，跨径16.2米，十一开间。东端建高大望楼，整桥为龙形。清嘉庆十年（1805年）、清道光十五年（1835年）、清同治三年（1864年）、清光绪二十年（1894年）、1936年复建。属于坪坦风雨桥，为全国重点文物保护单位。

Yongfu Bridge

Gaobu Village, Pingtan Township, Tongdao Dong Autonomous County, Hunan Province, built in 1785 AD.

Yongfu Bridge is a combined timber beam frame bridge with a *chuandou* style structure. Its beams are composed of logs, and it has a single span. It is connected by mortise and tenon technology without the use of a single iron nail. It is 39 meters long, 3.8 meters wide and has a span of 16.2 meters. Its gallery house has 11 bays. A tall building stands at the east end of the bridge. The whole bridge resembles a dragon. Yongfu Bridge has been restored and repaired in 1805 AD, 1835 AD, 1864 AD, 1894 AD, and 1936 AD. Yongfu Bridge is classified as Pingtan Wind and Rain Bridges, which have been listed as a major historical and cultural sites protected at the national level.

过路桥

湖南省通道侗族自治县，清代（1644—1911 年）

独孔叠木平梁全木结构廊桥，长 38 米、宽 3.5 米、高 6.5 米，顶部中段、东端建有双重檐阁楼，具有侗族建筑典型特征。桥堍建筑较大不设桥墩，桥面外侧设置一层木椽瓦顶雨披，专为保护底梁圆木免遭雨水侵蚀。廊道一侧与高脚屋相连，守桥人家居住。

Guolu Bridge

Tongdao Dong Autonomous County, Hunan Province, built during 1644-1911 AD.

This is a compound timber beam covered bridge with a single span. It is 38 meters long, 3.5 meters wide, and 6.5 meters high. Both the center and east end of the bridge have a pavilion with a double-eave roof that shows the distinctive features of Dong architecture. There is a relatively large bridge approach at either end, and the bridge is not supported by piers. A skirt made of timber rafters and tiles runs along the outside of the deck and protects the beam logs below from rain erosion. One side of the bridge's pathway is connected to a pile-supported house where people guarding the bridge live.

凉亭桥

湖南省龙山县洗车河镇,清乾隆四十五年(1780年)

湘西名镇洗车河地处红岩溪河与猛西河交汇口,原有大小两座廊桥,现仅存大桥改名凉亭桥。逢圩设市,廊桥里货摊鳞次栉比,镇民对此桥十分珍爱。《龙山县志》记:"大河桥系本埠乡绅肖家霖捐修,桥中廊柱、枋檩、坐凳、栏杆、檐板、面板以榫卯合成,无铁钉铁铆。"四墩三孔,平梁全木结构,长75米、宽4米、高10.5米。2012年大修,新建两座双飞檐四角阁塔、两座单飞檐六角阁亭。

Liangting Bridge

Xichehe Town, Longshan County, Hunan Province, built in 1780 AD.

The town of Xichehe is situated at the confluence of the Hongyanxi River and Mengxi River. Originally, there were two bridges, one big, the other small, but now only the bigger one remains. This was renamed as the Liangting Bridge. During regular market fairs, the bridge is filled with stalls, making the bridge much beloved by the townspeople. The *Longshan County Chronicle* records that "Xiao Jialin, a member of the local gentry, donated money to build Dahe Bridge. Its pillars, purlins, benches, railings, eaves, and boards are made of mortise and tenons without the use of iron nails or rivets." The timber bridge has four piers and three spans. It is a timber beam bridge, 75 meters long, 4 meters wide, and 10.5 meters high. In 2012, four new pavilions were added to the site, including two with four cornered roofs with double upturned eaves and two with six-cornered roofs with a single layer of upturned eaves.

壶圆桥

湖南省溆浦县葛竹坪镇,清同治四年(1865年)

又名双江桥、长亭子桥。两墩三孔,长45米,十四开间,桥墩上端三层井字枕木。原建有两座双层八角阁楼,现存一座。屈原在第二个放逐地溆浦县住过16年,"路漫漫其修远兮,吾将上下而求索",不正是他对彼岸的遥想吗?溆浦我没有走全,只流连于几座廊桥,却已经感触到山水的神妙与屈原的呼吸。因木构腐朽,桥体损毁严重,2021年7月25日被拆除,引起网民热议。

Huyuan Bridge

Gezhuping Town, Xupu County, Hunan Province, built in 1865 AD.

This bridge is also known as the Shuangjiang Bridge and Changtingzi Bridge. It has two piers and three spans, and is 45 meters long. The gallery house has 14 bays. A criss-cross pattern of timber cross-ties consisting of three layers, forming the shape of the Chinese character for well (井) are played on the upper ends of the piers to support the bridge. The bridge formerly had a pair of two-layer pavilions with eight-corner roofs, but only one remains at present. The famed poet Qu Yuan spent 16 years in Xupu County, the second place where he was exiled. Qu Yuan once said "The road ahead is long and has no end; yet high and low I will search with my will unbending." This depicted his expectations about the future. Although I have not seen all of Xupu and have only been to a few of its covered bridges, I have experienced the charm of its landscape and the echoes of Qu Yuan. Due to the rotten wooden structure, the bridge was seriously damaged, and it was demolished on July 25, 2021, causing heated discussion among netizens.

长丰桥

湖南省新化县天门乡，清咸丰八年（1858年）

天门乡小学的学生上下学必过此廊桥，当地百姓称其为"学子桥"。逢圩日，廊桥成为交易中心，各种山货琳琅满目。独孔叠梁伸臂式廊桥，长60米、宽4米、高14米。桥廊全木结构，各构件榫卯衔扣，牢固坚实抗风力强。重檐顶覆乌黑鱼鳞瓦，两端设牌楼厅。于1934年、2005年修缮。

Changfeng Bridge

Tianmen Township, Xinhua County, Hunan Province, built in 1858 AD.

Elementary school students use the bridge to travel back and forth to school. Because of this, the bridge is also called the Xuezi Bridge. On market days, the eye is astounded by a wealth of mountain products arrayed on the covered bridge. The bridge has a single span and is a timber cantilever compound beam bridge. Its joins are made with mortise and tenon technology, and it has a very high degree of stability and wind resistance. The bridge is 60 meters long, 4 meters wide, and 14 meters high. Its double-eave roof is covered with jet-grey "fish-scale" tiles, and memorial arch gateways stand at either end. The bridge was repaired in 1934 AD and 2005.

肖家桥

湖南省安化县乐安镇横市村柳林溪，清乾隆四十九年（1784年）

全木结构廊桥，南北走向，长31米、宽3米、高9米，十四开间，一墩两孔叠木平梁、重檐小青瓦硬山顶。桥廊属穿斗式木架结构，南北桥厅上部加建小楼阁。为省级文物保护单位。

Xiaojia Bridge

Liulin Creek, Hengshi Village, Le'an Town, Anhua County, Hunan Province, built in 1784 AD.

This is a timber combined beam covered bridge. It runs from north to south and has one pier and two spans. It is 31 meters long, 3 meters wide and 9 meters high. With 14 bays, the gallery house is a *chuandou* style structure, replete with a double-eave and flush gable roof covered with small grey tiles. Small pavilions were built on top of the bridge halls at each end. The bridge has been listed as a historical and cultural sites protected at the provincial level.

清代 1644—1911年

晏家桥

湖南省安化县乐安镇横市村柳林溪，清乾隆（1736—1795年）

南北走向，长35米、宽4米、高9米，十一开间。一墩两孔、石墩叠枕、平梁搭连、穿斗结构、歇山重檐、瓦顶廊桥。桥北端建有住房、店铺、灶房，南端加建楼阁式廊厅。因风雨侵蚀严重，清道光二十九年（1849年）修缮。

Yanjia Bridge

Liulin Creek, Hengshi Village, Le'an Town, Anhua County, Hunan Province, built during 1736-1795 AD.

Yanjia Bridge runs from north to south, is 35 meters long, 4 meters wide and 9 meters high. This is a timber beam *chuandou* style structure covered bridge. It has stone piers and layered cross-ties which together with connected beams form its main structure. It has one pier and two spans. Its gallery house has 11 bays and is topped by a multiple-eave and hip and gable roof covered with tiles. There are dwellings, shops, and a kitchen on the north end of the bridge. On the south end, there is a pavilion-style hall. Due to severe erosion caused by wind and rain, the bridge was repaired in 1849 AD.

燕子桥

湖南省安化县梅城镇启安社区，清乾隆（1736—1795年）

清道光二年（1822年）整修，一墩两孔圆木平梁全木结构廊桥，长38.5米、宽3.8米、高11米，十一开间，悬山重檐小青瓦顶，悬臂挑梁式木结构廊架。属于安化风雨桥，为全国重点文物保护单位。

Yanzi Bridge

Qi'an Community, Meicheng Town, Anhua County, Hunan Province, built during 1736-1795 AD.

Yanzi Bridge is a timber log cantilever beam bridge with one pier and two spans. It was renovated in 1822 AD. It is 38.5 meters long, 3.8 meters wide, and 11 meters high. Its gallery house has 11 bays. It has an overhanging gable roof with multiple-eaves, covered with small grey tiles, cantilever beam type wooden structure gallery. Yanzi Bridge is classified as Anhua Wind and Rain Bridges, which have been listed as a major historical and cultural sites protected at the national level.

复古桥

湖南省安化县柘溪镇双桥村双桥溪,清光绪三十三年(1907年)

  复古桥长30.8米、宽3.8米、高6米,十三开间,两墩三孔重檐歇山顶、悬臂挑梁木结构廊桥。大桥一侧的小型石拱廊桥长8米,宽约4米。双桥情似姊妹,远近闻名。复古桥属于安化风雨桥,为全国重点文物保护单位。

Fugu Bridge

Shuangqiao Creek, Shuangqiao Village, Zhexi Town, Anhua County, Hunan Province, built in 1907 AD.

Fugu Bridge is a timber cantilever beam covered bridge with two piers and three spans, covered by a hip and gable roof with multiple eaves. It is 30.8 meters long, 3.8 meters wide, and 6 meters high. Its gallery house has 13 bays. The smaller stone arch bridge beside the larger one is 8 meters long and approximately 4 meters wide. The sister-like relationship between the two bridges is known near and far. Fugu Bridge is classified as Anhua Wind and Rain Bridges, which have been listed as a major historical and cultural sites protected at the national level.

普修桥

湖南省通道侗族自治县皇都村，清乾隆（1736—1795年）

侗族居住地古称"溪峒"，沟壑田畴四处是水。为"上避天水、下跨地水"，侗族人民创造了风雨廊桥，与鼓楼、萨坛合称侗族建筑三宝。四墩三孔宝塔式廊桥，长57.7米、宽4.2米，二十一开间，桥墩上叠架双层枕木承托圆木平梁。重檐长廊上建三座宝塔，中塔顶尖设朱雀风向标。清嘉庆八年（1803年）山洪骤发被毁后重修。

Puxiu Bridge

Huangdu Village, Tongdao Dong Autonomous County, Hunan Province, built during 1736-1795 AD.

In old times, settlements of the Dong nationality were called *xidong*. This referred to the fact that their settlements are surrounded on all sides by water in gullies and fields. In order to shield themselves from the rain above and to travel over rivers below, Dong nationality created fengyu covered bridges, one of their three treasured architectural structures, together with drum towers and (Goddess) Sa altars. This pagoda-style covered bridge has three spans and is 57.7 meters long and 4.2 meters wide. Its gallery house has 21 bays. Double-layered cross-ties are piled on top of the bridge's piers to support the bridge's log beams. There are three pagodas on the bridge, and the middle one is decorated with a wind vane in the shape of the Chinese mythical vermillion bird of the south. The bridge was rebuilt after a flash flood in 1803 AD.

廻龙桥

湖南省通道侗族自治县坪坦乡平日村，清乾隆二十六年（1761年）

伸臂梁、伸臂木拱组合廊桥，长63.01米、宽3.86米，两墩三孔，采用侗族传统工艺"木桩围栏固基法"修建。西段木拱拱跨19.4米，拱架两端以30°斜升三排杉圆枕木，逐层伸臂，平桥面铺设木板，形成上平下拱状；东段为悬臂式木构，梯级迭坐；两种结构组合架设，体现了侗族工匠的高超技艺。属于坪坦风雨桥，为全国重点文物保护单位。

Huilong Bridge

Pingri Village, Pingtan Township, Tongdao Dong Autonomous County, Hunan Province, built in 1761 AD.

The combined covered bridge of cantilever beam and cantilever wooden arch is 63.01 meters long and 3.86 meters wide, with two piers and three spans. It is built using the traditional Dong ethnic group technique of the "wooden pile fence foundation method". The wooden arch in the western section has a span of 19.4 meters, with three rows of cedar sleepers rising at a 30° angle at both ends of the arch frame, extending outwards layer by layer, and the bridge deck is covered with wooden planks to form a flat upper section and an arched lower section. The eastern section is a cantilevered wooden structure with a stepped design. The combination of two structures reflects the superb skills of the Dong craftsmen. Huilong Bridge is classified as Pingtan Wind and Rain Bridges, which have been listed as a major historical and cultural sites protected at the national level.

普济桥

湖南省通道侗族自治县坪坦乡坪坦村,清乾隆二十五年(1760年)

清光绪二十一年(1895年)复修,1914年维修。单孔伸臂式木拱廊桥,长31.5米、宽3.8米、跨径19.8米。伸臂木梁插在两端空心石墩内,压大卵石。属于坪坦风雨桥,为全国重点文物保护单位。

Puji Bridge

Pingtan Village, Pingtan Township, Tongdao Dong Autonomous County, Hunan Province, built in 1760 AD.

The bridge was restored in 1895 AD and repaired in 1914 AD. It is a cantilever arch covered bridge with a single-span. It is 31.5 meters long, 3.8 meters wide, and has a span of 19.8 meters. Its cantilevered timber beams are inserted in the hollow stone bridge piers at either end. Puji Bridge is classified as Pingtan Wind and Rain Bridges, which have been listed as a major historical and cultural sites protected at the national level.

金勾风雨桥

贵州省从江县往洞镇增盈村金勾寨，清顺治十二年（1655年）

金勾风雨桥于清光绪九年（1883年）水毁后重建，石墩平梁全木结构廊桥，长33.60米、宽4.75米。据碑记："金勾风雨桥位于金勾寨脚。原桥址建于村寨旁，多次毁于洪水，1992年村民集资重建迁至现址。穿斗式石墩廊桥建筑，一墩两孔结构。桥梁采用密布式简支梁，十七开间，中部为密檐四角攒尖顶结构。加装漏窗和斗拱，与两侧悬山顶桥楼遥相呼应，起到了突出冠冕的作用。其营造技艺精湛是研究侗族建筑工艺、科学文化的重要实物。"为全国重点文物保护单位。

Jingou Fengyu Bridge

Jingou Stockade, Zengying Village, Wangdong Town, Congjiang County, Guizhou Province, built in 1655 AD.

This bridge was rebuilt in 1883 AD after being destroyed by a flood. The bridge has stone piers and a timber-bridge structure. It is 33.6 meters long and 4.75 meters wide. According to an inscription on a stele, "this bridge was originally built at the foot of the village, but it was destroyed many times by floods. In 1992, villagers raised funds to relocate it to the present site. It is a *chuandou* timber covered bridge with stone piers. It has one pier and two spans and uses closely arranged beams to support the structure. Its gallery house has 17 bays. The central part of the bridge has a four-corner multiple-eave pyramidal roof structure. It is decorated with ornamental perforated windows and *dougong* bracket sets. It is bordered on either side by buildings with overhanging gable roofs. Due to its exquisite structure, this bridge is instrumental in research on the construction techniques and scientific culture of the Dong nationality." It has been listed as a major historical and cultural sites protected at the national level.

地坪风雨桥

贵州省黎平县地坪镇南江河，清光绪八年（1882年）

地坪风雨桥自古扼控贵东南通往湘西、桂北孔道。三座桥楼与桥廊不用一钉一铆，没有设计图纸，凭借侗族民间工匠的高超技艺建造。一墩两孔，长55.88米、宽3.85米、高11米，两孔净跨分别为13.77米和21.42米。1964年重建，1981年修复。2004年7月20日水毁，地坪乡乡民将28根大梁和73%的大构件找回，2009年按照古貌复建。

Diping Fengyu Bridge

Nanjiang River, Diping Town, Liping County, Guizhou Province, built in 1882 AD.

Diping Fengyu Bridge has been a vital node connecting southeast Guizhou with western Hunan and northern Guangxi. Its three pavilions and its gallery house were built by ethnic Dong craftsmen who, with their prodigious skills, completed the project without blueprints and without use of a single iron nail or rivet. The double-span bridge is 55.88 meters long, 3.85 meters wide, and 11 meters high. Its two spans are 13.77 meters and 21.42 meters respectively. It was rebuilt in 1964 and renovated in 1981. The bridge was knocked asunder by a flood on July 20, 2004, after which villagers were able to retrieve 28 of its displaced crossbeams and 73% of its large timber members. In 2009, the bridge was rebuilt according to its ancient appearance.

牙双花桥

贵州省黎平县雷洞瑶族水族乡牙双村，清代（1644—1911年）

牙双花桥是贵州省南下重要古通道，距离广西壮族自治区三江侗族自治县独峒乡5公里。独孔全木穿斗式结构，长16米、宽3米、高7米，中部建四重檐歇山顶望楼。

Yashuang Huaqiao Bridge

Yashuang Village, Leidong Yao and Shui Ethnic Township, Liping County, Guizhou Province, during 1644-1911 AD.

Yashuang Huaqiao Bridge is an important ancient road leading southward in Guizhou. It is 5 kilometers away from Dudong Township in the Sanjiang Dong Autonomous County of Guangxi Zhuang Autonomous Region. The bridge is a single-span timber *chuandou* style structure. It is 16 meters long, 3 meters wide, and 7 meters high. Its center has a viewing structure topped with a four-eave hip and gable roof.

岑管花桥

贵州省黎平县雷洞瑶族水族乡，清代（1644—1911 年）

岑管花桥始建于清代，屡有毁建。桥长 35 米、宽 4 米。2004 年 7 月 20 日水毁，于 2005 年 8 月修复。

Cenguan Huaqiao Bridge

Leidong Yao and Shui Ethnic Township, Liping County, Guizhou Province, built during 1644-1911 AD.

Cenguan Huaqiao Bridge was first built in the Qing Dynasty (1644-1911 AD) and has been damaged and repaired many times. The bridge is 35 meters long and 4 meters wide. It was swept away by a flood on July 20, 2004, and was rebuilt in August, 2005.

翠谷桥

贵州省黎平县雷洞瑶族水族乡亚跨村，清代（1644—1911 年）

屡有修缮，因坐落于叠翠山谷得名，位于黎平县雷洞瑶族水族乡亚跨村偏僻处。独孔双层平梁全木结构廊桥，长 15.7 米、宽 2.8 米、高 5.2 米，是连通桂北、贵南古通道的必经节点。

Cuigu Bridge

Yakua Village, Leidong Yao and Shui Ethnic Township, Liping County, Guizhou Province, built during 1644-1911 AD.

Cuigu Bridge gets its name from its location in the Diecui Valley. It has been renovated many times. It is located in a remote area of the village; it is a timber beam covered bridge with a single span and two layers of beams. It is 15.7 meters long, 2.8 meters wide, and 5.2 meters high. It is an intersection of the ancient road that connected northern Guangxi to southern Guizhou.

村尾花桥

贵州省从江县往洞镇，清代（1644—1911年）

独孔石拱加立柱，石墩设置副孔，全木结构穿斗式廊桥，长28.2米、宽2.9米、高5.3米，十五开间，单脊双坡顶覆盖小青瓦，两端建有门厅。

Cunwei Huaqiao Bridge

Wangdong Town, Congjiang County, Guizhou Province, built during 1644-1911 AD.

Cunwei Huaqiao Bridge is a stone arch covered bridge with a completely timber gallery house on top consisting of a *chuandou* style structure. A secondary hole is carved into the bridge's stone pier. It is 28.2 meters long, 2.9 meters wide, and 5.3 meters high. Its gallery house has 15 bays. Its double-sloped roof is covered with small grey tiles, and entrance halls are erected at either end.

巩福桥

广西壮族自治区三江侗族自治县独峒镇独峒村，清光绪三年（1877年）

《巩福桥修复志》碑记节录："我侗民族崇尚礼仪，热心公益。故村寨中必设议事鼓楼，溪河上定架风雨花桥。构筑技艺超绝，美名饮誉中外。向者八协故有风雨桥一座，始建于清光绪三年（1877年）。是时建桥先人父老含辛茹苦，开凿山石筑基两台双墩，斫伐良木造桥四楼重檐，经营十有三载精工细作。桥长二十四丈，雄伟壮观。桥之建成民安乐，故命名巩福桥。"

Gongfu Bridge

Dudong Village, Dudong Town, Sanjiang Dong Autonomous County, Guangxi Zhuang Autonomous Region, built in 1877 AD.

It is recorded on the stele *Restoration of the Gongfu Bridge* that "We Dong Nationality strongly uphold propriety and deeply value the public welfare. As a result, the village had to install a drum tower in its center for public meetings, as well as erect a fengyu huaqiao bridge on the banks of the river. The structure was built with impeccable craftsmanship and is famous both near and far. Since old times, Baxie Village has had a fengyu bridge. It was first built in 1877 AD. At that time, the villagers building the bridge endured bitter hardship and chiseled two abutments and two piers out of the mountain rock for the bridge's foundation. They chopped down fine wood to construct the bridge's four buildings covered by roofs with multiple eaves. It was built through 13 years of excellent and careful work. The bridge is 24 *zhang* long and is magnificent and grand. The bridge's construction brought peace and happiness to the people, and as a result, its name is Gongfu Bridge."

岜团桥

广西壮族自治区三江侗族自治县独峒村岜团寨苗江，
清光绪二十四年（1898年）

岜团桥是连通湘西、桂北、黔南的交通要道，往来官民甚多。为避免牲畜惊吓、误伤老少妇孺与过往行人，营造安全整洁的环境，乡民公议多捐银两，聘请侗族梓匠（建筑大师）石含章、吴金添设计建造了中国独一无二的"立交式"风雨桥。东西走向，一墩两孔平梁、楼殿式全木结构，上层人行道高2.4米、宽4米，下层畜行道高1.9米、宽1.4米，全长50米。人畜通道分为两层，故称立交桥。三座楼阁五层重檐歇山顶，高8米。为全国重点文物保护单位。

Batuan Bridge

MiaoJiang River, Batuan Stockade, Dudong Village, Sanjiang Dong Autonomous County, Guangxi Zhuang Autonomous Region, built in 1898 AD.

Batuan Bridge was an important intersection connecting west Hunan, north Guangxi, and south Guizhou. In the past, because a large number of people came and went on the bridge, villagers collected money and invited Shi Hanzhang and Wu Jintian, two Dong architects, to design a bridge that could lessen the number of people injured by livestock along the bridge while at the same time maintaining a more clean environment along its length. Hence, this unique interchange-type fengyu bridge was designed and built. The bridge runs from east to west. It has one pier and two spans, and beams support the main bridge structure. It is a palace-style bridge, and is 50 meters in total. The upper passage for people is 2.4 meters high and 4 meters wide, and the one below for livestock is 1.9 meters high and 1.4 meters wide. The separation of people and livestock into an upper and lower corridor led to calling the structure an interchange bridge. There are three five-story pavilions on the bridge, which are each 8 meters high and sport multiple-eave and hip and gable roofs. Batuan Bridge has been listed as a major historical and cultural sites protected at the national level.

虹饮桥

广西壮族自治区全州县龙水镇龙水村万乡河，清乾隆（1736—1795 年）

《全州县志》记："全州县位于中原通岭南要道，系越头楚尾之地，得楚、中原文化之先。境内有清乾隆年间修建的虹饮桥，系县内有名古建筑。县内工匠多为湖南、江西等省流寓客匠。"五墩六孔全木结构平梁、木瓦砖石结构廊桥，长 72 米、宽 4.2 米、高 7 米，中部设重檐挑角小阁。红廊碧瓦如"彩虹饮水"得名。1998 年重修。

Hongyin Bridge

Wanxiang River, Longshui Village, Longshui Town, Quanzhou County, Guangxi Zhuang Autonomous Region, built during 1736-1795 AD.

The *Quanzhou County Chronicle* states that "Quanzhou County is located in the south of the Central Plains to the south of Five Ridges. It is where the ancient states of Yue and Chu share a border and was the earliest region to acquire the culture of the state of Chu and of the Central Plains. In Quanzhou County, there is a bridge built during the reign of Qianlong of the Qing Dynasty, which is famous throughout the county. Many of the craftsmen in the county were guest laborers from Hunan and Jiangxi." It has five piers and six spans. It is a timber, tile, brick, and stone structured covered bridge, with its main structure supported by timber beams. It is 72 meters long, 4.2 meters wide, and 7 meters high. There is a small pavilion with a multiple-eave roof with upturned corners in its center. The combination of the red gallery house and its jade colored tiles resembles "a rainbow drinking water", thus resulting in the bridge's name. In 1998, the bridge was rebuilt.

东辕桥

广西壮族自治区富川瑶族自治县朝东镇蚌贝村，
清乾隆三十四年（1769年）

独孔石平梁、青砖桥面、穿斗式结构、殿宇式廊桥，长15.6米、宽5.5米、高9米，五开间。单脊双坡顶建敞阔歇山顶阁楼，覆盖小青瓦，马头墙桥头。属于富川瑶族风雨桥群，为全国重点文物保护单位。

Dongyuan Bridge

Bangbei Village, Chaodong Town, Fuchuan Yao Autonomous County, Guangxi Zhuang Autonomous Region, built in 1769 AD.

This is a single span stone beam palace-style covered bridge and it is a *chuandou* style structure. Its deck is covered with grey bricks. The bridge is 15.6 meters long, 5.5 meters wide, and 9 meters high. The gallery house has 5 bays and has a single-ridge open hip and gable roof with double slopes, decorated with small grey tiles. At the entrance there is a horse-head wall. Dongyuan Bridge is classified as Fuchuan Yao Ethnicity Wind and Rain Bridges Cluster, which has been listed as a major historical and cultural sites protected at the national level.

环涧桥

广西壮族自治区富川瑶族自治县朝东镇长塘村，清道光二十二年（1842年）

环涧桥位于长塘村田野小溪，用于村民下田耕种避雨。两墩三孔、平梁砖墙、木柱瓦顶、通天阁楼式廊桥，长9.8米、宽3.9米、高8.6米、跨径8.96米，三开间。穿斗式结构，歇山顶桥亭，马头墙桥头。属于富川瑶族风雨桥群，为全国重点文物保护单位。

Huanjian Bridge

Changtang Village, Chaodong Town, Fuchuan Yao Autonomous County, Guangxi Zhuang Autonomous Region, built in 1842 AD.

Huanjian Bridge spans a stream that runs through an open field in Changtang Village. Villagers use it when farming to find shelter from the rain. The bridge was built as a covered bridge with beam supports, and it had two piers and three spans. Its gallery house was covered with brick walls and timber columns. The *chuandou* style structure gallery house has 3 bays and is covered by tiles. It is connected to a pavilion building with a hip and gable roof. It is 9.8 meters long, 3.9 meters wide, 8.6 meters high, and has a span of 8.96 meters. The bridge entrances have horse-head walls. Huanjian Bridge is classified as Fuchuan Yao Ethnicity Wind and Rain Bridges Cluster, which has been listed as a major historical and cultural sites protected at the national level.

双溪桥

广西壮族自治区富川瑶族自治县朝东镇东水村，清光绪十一年（1885年）

位于山村水口，两墩三孔、圆木平梁亭阁式廊桥，长20.8米、宽4.40米、高8米，跨径17米，七开间。桥面铺木板，穿斗式结构，桥廊和桥阁覆盖小青瓦，马头墙桥头。属于富川瑶族风雨桥群，为全国重点文物保护单位。

Shuangxi Bridge

Dongshui Village, Chaodong Town, Fuchuan Yao Autonomous County, Guangxi Zhuang Autonomous Region, built in 1885 AD.

The bridge is located at the place where this mountain village meets the water, it has two piers and three spans. It is supported by log beams and is a pavilion style covered bridge, *chuandou* style structure. It is 20.8 meters long, 4.40 meters wide, and 8 meters high. The bridge has a span of 17 meters, and its gallery house has 7 bays. The deck is covered with wooden boards. The gallery house and pavilions are covered with small grey tiles, and the entrance ways have horse-head walls. Shuangxi Bridge is classified as Fuchuan Yao Ethnicity Wind and Rain Bridges Cluster, which has been listed as a major historical and cultural sites protected at the national level.

钟灵桥

广西壮族自治区富川瑶族自治县朝东镇福溪村,清光绪三十年（1904年）

两墩三孔、石墙木柱、平梁瓦顶、歇山顶阁楼式廊桥,长10.6米、宽4.35米、高10米、跨径9.10米,三开间。桥面铺木板,穿斗式结构。桥头三块高大狰狞的石头,当地百姓称为"扎根石",为中国廊桥景观独有。据村老讲:"是地下龙王三片鳞甲保佑村寨的。上下桥不那么方便但我们从不介意,老少妇孺皆视如珍宝。外乡人用力拍几下我们都心痛。"属于富川瑶族风雨桥群,为全国重点文物保护单位。

Zhongling Bridge

Fuxi Village, Chaodong Town, Fuchuan Yao Autonomous County, Guangxi Zhuang Autonomous Region, built in 1904 AD.

This is a timber beam supported bridge with two piers and three spans; its piers are made of stone. The bridge is built in the style of a pavilion building with a *xieshanding* hip and gable roof, covered with tiles. It is 10.6 meters long, 4.35 meters wide, 10 meters high, and has a clear span of 9.10 meters. It has a gallery house with 3 bays. The bridge deck is covered with wooden boards, and it is a *chuandou* style structure. Three rugged natural giant stones have been preserved at the bridge entrance, which are called "root stones" by locals, something unique to covered bridges in China. According to the old people in the village, these stones are "three pieces of the underground dragon king's scaled armor, which serve to protect the village. The villagers, young and old, regard the stones as a real treasure; how strangers treat them makes us feel sad." Zhongling Bridge is classified as Fuchuan Yao Ethnicity Wind and Rain Bridges Cluster, which has been listed as a major historical and cultural sites protected at the national level.

仁安桥

浙江省松阳县玉岩镇周安村,清康熙(1662—1722年)

单孔木平梁、全木结构廊桥,五开间,重檐歇山顶满铺小青瓦,长12米、宽3米、高4.2米。古为村民进出大山唯一通道,也是耕种时节人们躲避风雨、休息闲谈的场所。

Ren'an Bridge

Zhouan Village, Yuyan Town, Songyang County, Zhejiang Province, built during 1662-1722 AD.

This is a timber beam bridge supported with a timber structure. It has a single span. Its gallery house has 5 bays. This is covered with a hip and gable roof with multiple eaves, topped with small grey tiles. The bridge is 12 meters long, 3 meters wide, and 4.2 meters high. In ancient times, it was the only way for villagers to go to and from the mountains. It was also a place for people to escape the wind and rain and to rest and have a chat during the farming season.

红军桥

浙江省松阳县安民乡安岱后村安民溪，清光绪（1875—1908年）

原名善继桥，始建于清光绪（1875—1908年）年间。单孔木平梁廊桥，长27.8米、宽5.4米，跨径5.5米，九开间。碑记："安岱后地处闽、浙、赣边界的浙江西南部，此处崇山峻岭，古木参天，万顷猴头杜鹃堪称华东一绝。1935年5月，中国工农红军挺进师在粟裕、刘英的率领下，依托安岱后战略要地建立了浙西南革命根据地。"1997年3月，萧克将军题写的"红军桥"碑立于桥头西侧。

Hongjun Bridge

Anmin Creek, Andaihou Village, Anmin Township, Songyang County, Zhejiang Province, built during 1875-1908 AD.

The bridge formerly known as Shanji Bridge, was built during the Emperor Guangxu reign of the Qing Dynasty (1875-1908 AD). It is a timber beam supported covered bridge. The bridge has one span and is 27.8 meters long, 5.4 meters wide, and has a span of 5.5 meters. Its gallery house has 9 bays. It stele states, "Andaihou is located in the southwestern part of Zhejiang Province on the border of Fujian, Zhejiang and Jiangxi, where the mountains are high and the ancient trees tower above, and ten thousand hectares of rhododendron simiarum make it known as one of the best lands in East China. In May 1935 AD, the Chinese Workers' and Peasants' Red Army Advancement Division under the command of Su Yu and Liu Ying created a revolutionary base area in Southwest Zhejiang Province on the basis of its strategic stronghold in Andaihou." In March 1997, General Xiao Ke's writing "Hongjun Bridge" was installed on the west side of the bridge entrance.

通洲桥

浙江省兰溪市梅江镇聚仁村梅溪，清康熙二十五年（1686年）

通洲桥古为金华、兰溪、义乌、浦江、建德五县交通咽喉。初为木桥，清乾隆二十三年（1758年）改石桥。清嘉庆五年（1800年）水毁，清道光三年（1823年）重建石拱廊桥。长85米、宽4米、高9米，四墩五孔，单孔跨径9米，二十一开间，是浙江省最大的石拱廊桥。两端建重檐歇山顶门楼，中部建重檐歇山顶阁楼。门梁木雕为清代匠师作品。

Tongzhou Bridge

Meixi Creek, Juren Village, Meijiang Town, Lanxi, Zhejiang Province, built in 1686 AD.

In ancient times, Tongzhou Bridge served as a node for traffic from Jinhua, Lanxi, Yiwu, Pujiang, and Jiande counties. At first, it was a timber bridge, and in 1758 AD it was converted into a stone bridge. In 1800 AD, it was destroyed by floods, and in 1823 AD it was rebuilt as a stone arch bridge. It is 85 meters long, 4 meters wide, and 9 meters high. It has four piers and five spans, with a single span 9 meters long. Its gallery house has 21 bays. It is the largest stone arch bridge in Zhejiang Province. Both sides of the bridge have memorial archways covered by multiple-eave hip and gable roofs. In the center, there is a pavilion, also with a multiple-eave hip and gable roof. The wood carving on the beam by the bridge's entrance is the work of master craftsmen of the Qing Dynasty.

戈场桥

浙江省平阳县顺溪镇戈场村，清康熙四十年（1701年）

又名永安桥，初为全木结构木拱廊桥。清道光（1821—1850年）年间改建为独孔石拱廊桥，长23米、宽5米。1961年修缮。20世纪90年代，上部木结构被焚毁，1993年重建。2007年被强台风损毁，2010年重建。桥北连通千步岭古道，现已荒芜难行。

Gechang Bridge

Gechang Village, Shunxi Town, Pingyang County, Zhejiang Province, built in 1701 AD.

Gechang Bridge, also known as Yongan Bridge, was a timber arch covered bridge originally. Sometime between 1821 AD and 1850 AD, it was rebuilt as a stone arch bridge with a single span. It is 23 meters long and 5 meters wide. In 1961, it was repaired. In the early 1990s, the bridge's upper timber structure burned down and was rebuilt in 1993. The bridge was destroyed by a strong typhoon in 2007 and was rebuilt in 2010. The ancient Qianbuling Road that connects to the north side of the bridge has become overgrown and now is difficult to access.

慕义桥

浙江省缙云县前路乡前路村，清道光十二年（1832年）

慕义桥长53米、宽3.4米、高7米，三孔跨径各8.7米，各方集资一万三千两白银历时一年建成。桥栏刻字"慕义桥，道光十二年，缙云县令张惟孝书"。西端桥亭高11.22米，北厢为庙、西厢为亭，六开间。慕义桥构造精湛，是缙云县有确切纪年并保存完好的石拱廊桥，具有较高的历史、文化、艺术和科学价值。为省级文物保护单位。

Muyi Bridge

Qianlu Village, Qianlu Township, Jinyun County, Zhejiang Province, built in 1832 AD.

The Muyi Bridge is 53 meters long, 3.4 meters wide, and 7 meters high. Each of its spans is 8.7 meters long. It was built through various contributions totaling 13,000 taels of silver and was completed in one year's time. An engraving on the bridge's railing states, "Muyi Bridge, built in 1832 AD, signed by *Xianling* (County Magistrate) Zhang Weixiao." The pavilion on the bridge's western end is 11.22 meters high. The bridge's northern chamber serves as a temple, and its western chamber is a pavilion, and its gallery house has 6 bays. Muyi Bridge has an exquisite structure, It is the best-preserved stone arch covered bridge in Jinyun County, whose built year was ascertained, with high historical, cultural, artistic and scientific value. The bridge has been listed as a historical and cultural sites protected at the provincial level.

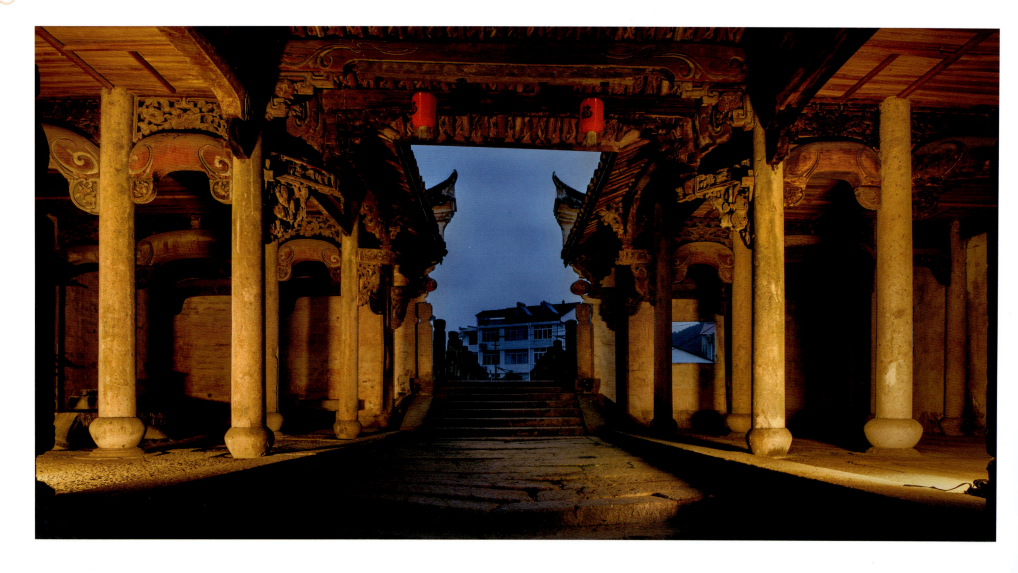

双溪桥

浙江省龙泉市小梅镇孙坑村，清同治十年（1871年）

  1932年重建。叠木平梁辅助八字支撑，全木结构廊桥，东南—西北走向，长32.6米、宽4.5米、高3.75米，跨径15.4米，十一开间。重檐单脊廊顶，中央建双檐翘角歇山顶小阁楼，内设神龛供奉观世音菩萨。为省级文物保护单位。

Shuangxi Bridge

Sunkeng Village, Xiaomei Town, Longquan, Zhejiang Province, built in 1871 AD.

In 1932 AD, Shuangxi Bridge was rebuilt. It is a timber covered bridge supported by compound timber beams, together with auxiliary *bazi* bracing. It runs from the southeast to the northwest. It is 32.6 meters long, 4.5 meters wide, and 3.75 meters high. It has a span of 15.4 meters, and a gallery house with 11 bays. The gallery house has a multiple-eave single-ridge roof. In its center, there is a small pavilion with a hip and gable roof with double-eave and upturned corners. Inside it is a shrine built for the public's worship of Guan Yin, the Buddhist bodhisattva of compassion. It has been listed as a historical and cultural sites protected at the provincial level.

黄水长桥

浙江省庆元县百山祖镇黄水村，清乾隆十九年（1754年）

又名飞阁桥。清同治十一年（1872年）迁建到现址。2003年因修建水电站整体抬升1.7米，单孔全木结构伸臂式廊桥，南北走向，长54.3米、宽4.90米、高8.70米，跨径17.45米，二十一开间。桥拱依托石砌桥塊，粗大贯木穿插别压组接拱架，上建廊屋，弧形硬山顶覆青杂瓦，两侧三叠木质雨披，引桥占整座廊桥的三分之二。属于处州廊桥，为全国重点文物保护单位。

Huangshui Changqiao Bridge

Huangshui Village, Baishanzu Town, Qingyuan County, Zhejiang Province, built in 1754 AD.

The bridge, also called Feige Bridge, was moved to the present location in 1872 AD. The bridge was raised by an additional 1.7 meters when a hydroelectric power station was built at its location in 2003. The single-span cantilever beam bridge stretches from north to south, and it is 54.3 meters long, 4.90 meters wide, and 8.70 meters high. Its gallery house has 21 bays, and it has a span of 17.45 meters. Its timber arch is supported by stone abutments. The thick wood is inserted to form the arch frame, on which there is a gallery house. The gallery house is covered by an arched flush gable roof with grey tiles, replete with three-layer awnings at each side. The approaches to the bridge occupy two thirds of the whole bridge. Huangshui Changqiao Bridge is classified as Chuzhou Covered Bridges, which have been listed as a major historical and cultural sites protected at the national level.

护龙桥

浙江省庆元县岭头乡杨家庄村,清嘉庆二十五年(1820年)

木平梁全木结构廊桥,长 27.75 米、宽 5.12 米、高 2.15 米,跨径 7 米,十一开间,双层木质雨披,悬山顶覆小青瓦。为省级文物保护单位。

Hulong Bridge

Yangjiazhuang Village, Lingtou Township, Qingyuan County, Zhejiang Province, built in 1820 AD.

Hulong Bridge is a covered bridge supported by timber beams with a wooden gallery house. It is 27.75 meters long, 5.12 meters wide, 2.15 meters high and has a span of 7 meters. It has a gallery house with 11 bays. A double-layer wooden awning protects the bridge from rain. The bridge is covered by an overhanging gable roof topped by small grey tiles. It has been listed as a historical and cultural sites protected at the provincial level.

畲桥

浙江省景宁畲族自治县东坑镇，清康熙三十一年（1692年）

古官名永安桥。长37.5米、宽5米，跨径29.2米，东西走向，为全木结构独孔木拱廊桥。该桥横跨白鹤溪，英姿挺拔，深受畲族人民喜爱，故改名为畲桥，以代表民族气质。清道光十二年（1832年）、清光绪二十年（1894年）整修。《景宁县志》描述畲桥"依壁如虹"。桥头遗存清道光（1821—1850年）功德碑、记事碑八方。

Sheqiao Bridge

Dongkeng Town, Jingning She Autonomous County, Zhejiang Province, built in 1692 AD.

Its ancient official name was the Yongan Bridge. It is 37.5 meters long, 5 meters wide, and has a span of 29.2 meters. It is a single-span timber woven arch-beam bridge, stretching from east to west. Crossing the Baihe Creek, its appearance is bold and heroic. Much beloved by the She nationality, its name was changed to the Sheqiao Bridge to represent the attributes of their people. It was renovated in 1832 AD and 1894 AD. As stated in the *History of Jingning County*, Sheqiao Bridge is "like a rainbow". Eight stone steles built during 1821-1850 AD are installed at the gateway to the bridge, recording good deeds and history related to the bridge.

回龙桥

浙江省景宁畲族自治县梧桐乡高演村，清乾隆（1736—1795年）

又名末尾桥。长21米、宽6米。明永乐（1403—1424年）年间，山村任家热心推崇勤耕苦读，族规"诗礼传家，书香踵接"。清乾隆至清光绪一百七十余年中数十户家庭的高演村，出贡生34人。某年村塾十名学子赴温州科考，九名考取，以"十学九贡"的声誉震惊朝野。之后，历届知县均到高演村连过三桥，以体味其中奥妙。

Huilong Bridge

Gaoyan Village, Wutong Township, Jingning She Autonomous County, Zhejiang Province, built during 1736-1795 AD.

Huilong Bridge is also known as the Mowei Bridge. It is 21 meters long and 6 meters wide. People in the village were known as industrious farmers and scholars, with a lineage principle that "culture should be passed through the generations and reading should be an unceasing practice" during 1403-1424 AD. During the over 170 years from the Qianlong to the Guangxu periods in the Qing Dynasty, 34 people in this small village of only several dozen households became *gongsheng*, who were then eligible to sit for the provincial or national exams. Once ten students from the village attended the state exams in Wenzhou, and nine of them passed them, astounding people near and far. After this, every magistrate of the county would walk over the three bridges in Gaoyan Village to experience this place's tradition and success.

环胜桥

浙江省景宁畲族自治县梧桐乡高演村，清乾隆七年（1742 年）

又名顶头桥，廊屋长 30.6 米、宽 5.65 米，跨径 3.55 米，十一开间，数根粗大杉木承载桥体，属独孔平梁全木结构楼阁式廊桥。桥楼三层，一层阔大廊屋为村学课堂，二层设文昌阁兼师爷住所，三层是四角挑檐悬山顶魁星楼。两端各有通道走廊，连接龙泉市通往温州的沿海古道。属于处州廊桥，为全国重点文物保护单位。

Huansheng Bridge

Gaoyan Village, Wutong Township, Jingning She Autonomous County, Zhejiang Province, built in 1742 AD.

Also named Dingtou Bridge, the gallery house is 30.6 meters long, 5.65 meters wide, and has a span of 3.55 meters. Its gallery house has 11 bays. It is a single-span covered bridge with its main structure supported by timber beams. Its gallery house includes a three-story pavilion. The first floor served as a classroom for villagers; the second floor as a room for teachers as well as a shrine dedicated to *wenquxing* (the Taoist god of art and literature); and the third floor is a pavilion for *kuixing* (the Taoist god of examinations). The structure is covered by an overhanging gable roof with four-corner upturned eaves. There are covered passageways at both ends that served the ancient road that connected Longquan County and the coastal areas of Wenzhou. Huansheng Bridge is classified as Chuzhou Covered Bridges, which have been listed as a major historical and cultural sites protected at the national level.

护关桥

浙江省景宁畲族自治县大漈乡,清乾隆四十六年（1781年）

　　长27米、宽6.5米、高8.5米,九开间,为悬山顶三层重檐、一墩两孔平梁廊桥。桥屋一层关帝庙、二层文昌阁、三层魁星楼,通道宽度不足2米。桥侧古色古香的时思寺,建于南宋绍兴十年（1140年）。

Huguan Bridge

Daji Village, Jingning She Autonomous County, Zhejiang Province, built in 1781 AD.

The bridge has one pier and two spans, and its main structure is supported by timber beams. It is 27 meters long, 6.5 meters wide, 8.5 meters high. Its gallery house has 9 bays. The bridge is covered by an overhanging gable roof with a triple-eave. The first floor of the pavilion serves as a shrine for Emperor Guanyu (a general during the Three Kindoms period), the second for *wenquxing* (the Taoist god of art and literature), and the third for *kuixing* (the Taoist god of examinations). The passageway of the pavilion is less than 2 meters wide. There is a temple named Shisi besides the bridge, which was built in 1140 AD.

大赤坑桥

浙江省景宁畲族自治县大均乡，清嘉庆十五年（1810年）

又名大赤坑楼桥、成名桥。清道光二年（1822年）、清同治三年（1864年）、1923年整修。单孔伸臂式木拱廊桥，长36.4米、宽5米、跨径30米，十四开间。两侧安置遮雨护板，全木穿斗式构造，梁、柱、檩由卯榫衔接。单脊双披顶，中部置挑角飞檐小阁，覆小青瓦。大赤坑桥昔为景宁县至沙湾、英川、庆元县等地驿道津梁。属于处州廊桥，为全国重点文物保护单位。

Dachikeng Bridge

Dajun Township, Jingning She Autonomous County, Zhejiang Province, built in 1810 AD.

Dachikeng Bridge, also known as Dachikeng Louqiao Bridge or Chengming Bridge. It was renovated in 1822 AD, 1864 AD, and 1923 AD. The single-span timber cantilever arch covered bridge is 36.4 meters long, 5 meters wide, and has a span of 30 meters. It has a gallery house with 14 bays. Baffles run along both sides of the bridge to protect it from rain. The gallery house is a *chuandou* style structure, and its beams, columns, and purlins are joined by mortise and tenon technology. The single-ridge roof has two slopes, and there is a small pavilion in its center, which is decorated with upturned eaves and small grey tiles. The bridge connects the ancient courier road that ran from Jingning County to Shawan, Yingchuan, and Qingyuan counties. Dachikeng Bridge is classified as Chuzhou Covered Bridges, which have been listed as a major historical and cultural sites protected at the national level.

苇岱岭脚桥

浙江省景宁畲族自治县家地乡苇岱村,清同治九年（1870年）

伸臂式木拱廊桥,南北走向,跨石壁溪,长38米。2009年修缮。为县级文物保护单位。

Xiongdai Lingjiao Bridge

Xiongdai Village, Jiadi Township, Jingning She Autonomous County, Zhejiang Province, built in 1870 AD.

It is a covered bridge with an overhanging wooden arch. The north-south bridge spanning Shibi Creek is 38 meters long. It was repaired in 2009. It has been listed as a historical and cultural sites protected at the county level.

湖南亭桥

浙江省衢州市衢江区湖南镇湖南村，清乾隆（1736—1795年）

湖南亭桥受到村民珍惜呵护。一位避雨老人讲："20世纪初，湖南亭桥办过私塾。其实有大房子用，教书的女先生就喜欢这里，说这座桥'恰似家女绣花楼'。"叠梁单孔红柱花窗，平梁全木结构廊桥，长13.5米、宽2米，七开间，廊柱间花格窗棂工艺精细考究。清同治十二年（1873年）重建。

Hunan Tingqiao Bridge

Hunan Village, Hunan Town, Qujiang District, Quzhou, Zhejiang Province, built during 1736-1795 AD.

This bridge is cherished by villagers. An old man who took shelter from the rain here said, "At the beginning of the 20th Century, the bridge was used as a private school. In fact, there was a large building for school use. The women who taught here liked this bridge a lot, saying that it was like a girl's embroidery." The bridge is formed from compound beams and has a single span. Its gallery house has red columns and decorative windows. Its main structure is supported by beams. The bridge is 13.5 meters long and 2 meters wide. Its gallery house has 7 bays. The lattice windows between the columns in the gallery house are exquisitely and delicately crafted. The bridge was reconstructed in 1873 AD.

清代 1644—1911年

北涧桥

浙江省泰顺县泗溪镇下桥村，清康熙十三年（1674年）

北涧桥一身红装如彩蝶舞翅，在古桥研究界、众多中外游客中有"中国最美廊桥"的评价。长51.7米、宽5.37米、跨径29米，二十九开间，歇山顶正中建重檐楼阁。属于泰顺廊桥，为全国重点文物保护单位。

Beijian Bridge

Xiaqiao Village, Sixi Town, Taishun County, Zhejiang Province, built in 1674 AD.

Beijian Bridge, which looks like a butterfly flapping its wings from a distance, is acclaimed as the most beautiful covered bridge in China by scholars of ancient bridges and by tourists from home and abroad. It is 51.7 meters long and 5.37 meters wide, with a span of 29 meters. Its gallery house has 29 bays. The bridge has a hip and gable roof. In the middle of the bridge there is a pavilion with multiple eaves. Beijian Bridge is classified as Taishun Covered Bridges, which have been listed as a major historical and cultural sites protected at the national level.

霞光桥

浙江省泰顺县泗溪镇，清雍正元年（1723年）

又名下洋桥。单孔石拱木屋廊桥，长17.26米、宽4.42米，拱券高7.3米，跨径13.2米，七开间，二重檐悬山顶覆薄灰瓦。初为木拱廊桥，因乡民用火不慎多次焚毁。清雍正（1723—1735年）、清咸丰（1851—1861年）年间多次重建。清代晚期，村社望耆召集村众"议者不利于木思易以石，虽计费倍之，然木不如石之安且久也"。四方百姓广捐资财，最终"砌以石，而仍屋之"，改建为独孔石拱木屋廊桥。属于泰顺廊桥，为全国重点文物保护单位。

Xiaguang Bridge

Sixi Town, Taishun County, Zhejiang Province, built in 1723 AD.

Also known as Xiayang Bridge, this single-span stone arch covered bridge with a timber gallery house is 17.26 meters long, 4.42 meters wide, with an arch height of 7.3 meters, and a span of 13.2 meters. Its gallery house has 7 bays. Its double-eave overhanging gable roof is covered by thin grey tiles. The bridge burned down several times due to accidents by villagers. It was reconstructed many times during 1723-1735 AD and 1851-1861 AD. In the late Qing Dynasty, after a discussion called for by the elders in the village, it was decided that despite representing an extra expense, stone would be safer to use than timber. Donations for the project came from near and far. In the end stone was used for the masonry of the bridge, forming a single-span stone arch covered bridge. However, its roof was still built with timber. Xiaguang Bridge is classified as Taishun Covered Bridges, which have been listed as a major historical and cultural sites protected at the national level.

永庆桥

浙江省泰顺县三魁镇，清嘉庆二年（1797年）

清道光二十二年（1842年）重建。独墩两孔伸臂式木拱廊桥，长33米、宽4.5米，十二开间。桥墩青石叠砌，上置两层长梁圆木支托桥体，桥面铺有宽木板，内有扶梯可供上下，两侧设置防雨木板，歇山顶覆小青瓦，正中建双层飞檐阁楼。属于泰顺廊桥，为全国重点文物保护单位。

Yongqing Bridge

Sankui Town, Taishun County, Zhejiang Province, built in 1797 AD.

The bridge was rebuilt in 1842 AD. It is a cantilever timber arch covered bridge. It has one pier and two spans. The bridge is 33 meters long and 4.5 meters wide. It has a gallery house with 12 bays. The bridge pier is made of stacked grey stones. Two long log beams are placed on the piers to support the bridge structure. The bridge deck is covered with timber planks. Stairs are installed on the bridge, allowing people to go up and down. Skirts run along both sides to protect the bridge from rain. The bridge has a hip and gable roof covered by small grey tiles, and in the middle of the bridge there is a two-story pavilion topped by a roof with upturned-eaves. Yongqing Bridge is classified as Taishun Covered Bridges, which have been listed as a major historical and cultural sites protected at the national level.

普宾桥

浙江省泰顺县雅阳镇，清嘉庆（1796—1820 年）

　　双木支柱平梁式全木结构廊桥，长 13.6 米、宽 4.25 米、高 3.74 米、跨径 8.54 米，是泰顺县通往东部邻县和福建省北部各县的重要津梁。当年建桥信息一经传播，得到泰顺县、平阳县、寿宁县、柘荣县等地百姓捐助。工程告竣后的节余银两在廊桥西端修建茶亭，供行人免费饮茶直到余款用尽。以"普天下皆宾客"之意取名普宾桥。

清代 1644—1911 年

Pubin Bridge

Yayang Town, Taishun County, Zhejiang Province, built during 1796-1820 AD.

This timber beam covered bridge supported by two wooden columns is 13.6 meters long, 4.25 meters wide, 3.74 meters high, and has a span of 8.54 meters. It serves as an important passageway running from Taishun County to the eastern adjacent counties and to the northern counties of Fujian Province. The construction of this bridge was funded by common people from Taishun County, Pingyang County, Shouning County, Zherong County, and other places who donated to the project as soon as news of the construction was received. After finishing the project, remaining funds were spent on building a tea-pagoda at the west end of the bridge to provide free tea to travelers until funds were exhausted. The bridge is named Pubin Bridge to signify that all people are welcome guests at this place.

毓文桥

浙江省泰顺县罗阳镇,清道光十九年(1839年)

1986年村民自筹资金修缮,桥长23米、宽4米、跨径7.6米,六开间,内设扶梯,为独孔石拱木结构廊桥。拱券式桥墩由青石筑砌,呈半月状横跨小山之间。上部结构为三层楼阁,屋顶为重檐歇山顶式样,屋脊正中有宝葫芦装饰,四翼飞檐翘角,桥屋二楼设立文昌阁。属于泰顺廊桥,为全国重点文物保护单位。

Yuwen Bridge

Luoyang Town, Taishun County, Zhejiang Province, built in 1839 AD.

The bridge is 23 meters long, 4 meters wide, and has a span of 7.6 meters. It has a single span and has a stone arch and a timber structure. Its gallery house has 6 bays. A ladder is installed inside the bridge. It was rebuilt in 1986 with funds collected by villagers. Its rolling-arch style bridge piers are composed of grey stone masonry, forming the shape of a crescent moon spanning the space between the hills. The upper part of the bridge has a three-story pavilion covered with a multiple-eave hip and gable roof with four wings and upturned eaves and winged corners. On the roof ridge sits a long-melon jewel decoration. The second story serves as a pavilion dedicated to *wenquxing* (the Taoist god of art and literature). Yuwen Bridge is classified as Taishun Covered Bridges, which have been listed as a major historical and cultural sites protected at the national level.

文兴桥

浙江省泰顺县筱村镇玉溪，清咸丰七年（1857年）

　　木拱廊桥长46.2米、宽5米、跨径29.6米，十六开间。北侧略高的桥屋供奉三座神像，上挂"灯火千秋"古匾。逢初一、十五乡民前来祭祀。有"守桥女神"之名的钟篮玉（畲族，1926年生），在老伴去世后，在桥北小屋住下。白天清扫轰赶畜禽，晚上掐灭香头烛火。涨大水前一定会召集乡亲抬来重物将桥身压稳。属于泰顺廊桥，为全国重点文物保护单位。

Wenxing Bridge

Yuxi Creek, Xiaocun Town, Taishun County, Zhejiang Province, built in 1857 AD.

It is a timber arch covered bridge, and it's 46.2 meters long, 5 meters wide, with a span of 29.6 meters. Its gallery house has 16 bays. Three statues of gods are enshrined in the north end of the bridge's gallery house (which is slightly higher than the others). An ancient plaque hangs from the bridge that reads "To Last for a Thousand Years". On the first and fifteenth days of the lunar new year, villagers come here to offer sacrifices. The bridge's guardian is Zhong Lanyu (She nationality, born in 1926 AD). She has lived in the house to the north of the bridge since her husband passed away. During the daytime, she sweeps the bridge and rids it of pests and animals. Before night, she extinguishes candles and incense on the bridge to prevent fires. During times of the flood, she will organize the villagers to place heavy objects on the bridge to stabilize it. Wenxing Bridge is classified as Taishun Covered Bridges, which have been listed as a major historical and cultural sites protected at the national level.

清代　1644—1911年

龙津桥

福建省屏南县屏城乡后龙村,清顺治(1644—1661年)

曾名玉锁桥、溪尾桥。东西走向,全木结构伸臂式木拱廊桥,长33.5米、宽4.5米,跨径23米,十三开间,九檩穿斗式构架支撑悬山顶式廊顶。桥东碑记:"子孙万世之业,永世原于实有功德,而功德莫大于造桥实济之为一也。余水尾厝桥水坏百余年重建,难再观矣。"

Longjin Bridge

Houlong Village, Pingcheng Township, Pingnan County, Fujian Province, built during 1644-1661 AD.

Once known as Yusuo Bridge and Xiwei Bridge. This timber cantilever arch bridge runs in an east to west direction. It is 33.5 meters long, 4.5 meters wide, and has a span of 23 meters. Its gallery house has 13 bays and is a *chuandou* style structure with nine purlins that support a flush gable roof. An inscription on the stele to the east of the bridge states that "The deeds of many generations originate from merit, and what merit is greater than that of building a bridge and striving together for this one purpose? After one hundred years of water damage, it was difficult to reconstruct the bridge."

赤岩虹桥

福建省周宁县泗桥乡赤岩村,清康熙四十一年(1702年)

原为木拱廊桥通古驿道。清嘉庆十六年(1811年),生员谢联元、吕振茂募资重建,仍为木拱廊桥。清光绪三十三年(1907年),乡绅谢春荣捐家财将其改建为石拱廊桥,坚牢稳固百余年无损。长27米、宽5米,九开间,高于河床30米。36根朱漆大柱支撑双层挑檐八角阁楼。

Chiyan Hongqiao Bridge

Chiyan Village, Siqiao Township, Zhouning County, Fujian Province, built in 1702 AD.

Originally, this was a timber arch covered bridge, leading to an ancient courier road. In 1811 AD, two members of the local literati who had passed the first level official examinations, Xie Lianyuan and Lv Zhenmao, raised funds to reconstruct the bridge, and it was remained a timber arch covered bridge. In 1907 AD, Xie Chunrong, a local gentry, donated his family's wealth to rebuild it as a stone arch bridge, which has remained firm and stable for over a hundred years without suffering any damage. It is 27 meters long, 5 meters wide, and has a gallery house with 9 bays. The bridge spans 30 meters above the riverbed. Thirty-six large columns covered in red lacquer support the two-story pavilion's octagonal roof and overhanging eaves.

岭兜桥

福建省寿宁县平溪镇岭兜村,清乾隆十九年(1754年)

清咸丰七年(1857年)重建。南北走向,独孔木平梁廊桥,长30米、宽4米,跨径6.5米,十一开间。两端桥堍大块青石砌筑,桥南端墙壁嵌石碑四方。岭兜桥一侧连通两间客栈。清代早期闽浙两省往来热络,桥旁有大小客栈36家。桥头客栈造饭锅灶已塌毁,灶王爷神像还在。

Lingdou Bridge

Lingdou Village, Pingxi Town, Shouning County, Fujian Province, built in 1754 AD.

The bridge was rebuilt in 1857 AD. This timber beam covered bridge has a single span and runs in a north-south direction. It is 30 meters long, 4 meters wide, with a span of 6.5 meters and has a gallery house with 11 bays. Both sides of the bridge are built with large grey stone masonry. The walls at the south end of the bridge have four stele encased within. Lingdou Bridge is connected with two inns. In the early Qing Dynasty, the bridge served as a much trafficked artery connecting Fujian and Zhejiang. It previously had 36 large and small inns beside it. While the large kitchen stove for the bridge's inns has been destroyed, a statue of the god of the kitchen remains.

清代 1644—1911年

升仙桥

福建省寿宁县犀溪镇仙锋村，清道光十九年（1839年）

东西走向，全木结构，独孔三重檐阁楼式廊桥，长26.8米、宽4米、跨径14.5米，九开间。建于清康熙四十一年（1702年）的永乐宫位于水尾，与升仙桥结为一体，村民称其为"水尾宫""官桥头"。

Shengxian Bridge

Xianfeng Village, Xixi Town, Shouning County, Fujian Province, built in 1839 AD.

The bridge has an east to west orientation and has a full timber structure. It has a single span and is a triple-eave-style pavilion. It is 26.8 meters long, 4 meters wide, and has a span of 14.5 meters. Its gallery house has 9 bays. The Yongle Temple, built in 1702 AD at the "water-tail" of the village is integrated into the Shengxian Bridge as one unit. The villagers call the structures the "water-tail temple" and the "temple's bridgehead" respectively.

馀庆桥

福建省武夷山市，清光绪（1875—1908 年）

《崇安县新志》记载："崇安（武夷山市）南郊阻大河行者病涉，（缙绅）敬熙（1852—1917 年）秉母命，以三万金创馀庆、垂裕二桥，雄伟为闽北冠"。抗日战争时期，垂裕桥毁于战火。馀庆桥西北东南走向，长 79 米、宽近 7 米、高 9 米，由长廊、亭阁、门楼、台阶、桥拱、桥墩组成。四座石墩脯顶安置长颈鸢，后放"压惊石"。2011 年 5 月 28 日，下午馀庆桥失火倒塌。2014 年 7 月，复建工程启动。属于闽东北廊桥，为全国重点文物保护单位。

Yuqing Bridge

Wuyishan, Fujian Province, built during 1875-1908 AD.

As it is recorded in the *New History of Chong'an County*, "people had a difficult time crossing the river in the southern suburb of Chong'an (now Wuyishan), so an official named Zhu Jingxi (1852-1917 AD), under the guidance of his mother, built two bridges named Yuqing and Chuiyu there with thirty thousand taels of silver. The magnificence of the bridges is known all around north Fujian Province." Chuiyu Bridge, however, was destroyed during the War of Resistance Against Japanese. Yuqing Bridge though remains, and stretches from northwest to southeast. It is 79 meters long, nearly 7 meters wide, and 9 meters high. It consists of a long gallery that includes pavilions, gateways, steps, arches, and piers. Sculptures of kite birds are installed on the four stone bow-shaped bridge piers. Yuqing Bridge collapsed in a fire in the afternoon of May 28, 2011. In July 2014, the reconstruction project of Yuqing Bridge was launched. Yuqing Bridge is classified as the Covered Bridges in the east and north of Fujian, which have been listed as a major historical and cultural sites protected at the national level.

清代 1644—1911 年

花桥

福建省松溪县花桥乡花桥村，清雍正（1723—1735年）

初为石墩杉木夹板桥，后水毁。清光绪三十一年（1905年），水北街镇乡绅吴观星倾其所有建造两墩三孔廊桥。村民张明浪介绍："修建花桥倾尽吴观星一家数代勤俭度日所余积蓄。以后每逢浦城人到花桥赶集卖东西，花桥乡民都会把路边最好的摊位让出来。"东西走向，石拱廊屋桥，长36米，十一开间，重檐歇山顶辅以单脊双坡顶马头墙桥口。桥孔、桥面使用长方形条石砌造，正中建造桥阁，内置四角藻井。

Huaqiao Bridge

Huaqiao Village, Huaqiao Township, Songxi County, Fujian Province, built during 1723-1735 AD.

Huaqiao Bridge was initially built with fir planks and stone piers and then was destroyed in a flood. In 1905 AD, Wu Guanxing, a member of the local gentry from Shuibeijie Town, contributed all he had to the construction of a two pier and three span covered bridge. The villager Zhang Minglang said, "Wu Guanxing spent all the money collected through generations for the construction of Huaqiao Bridge, so every time people from Pucheng (where Wu came from) came and sold goods on the bridge during market days, villagers of Huaqiao would give the best roadside stalls to them." The bridge's gallery house has 11 bays. It is 36 meters long and extends from east to west. It consists of a stone arch and is covered by a multiple-eave hip and gable roof. Its gateway also has a two-slope single ridge horse-head gable wall. The bridge's span and its deck are constructed with rectangular stones. In the bridge's center is a four-panel sunken *zaojing* caisson window.

乐丰桥

福建省浦城县临江镇水西村，清嘉庆十四年（1809 年）

四根木柱支撑圆木平梁，全木结构廊桥，重檐悬山顶，双层雨披。朱漆木柱，两端稍窄，中部两侧加宽。

Lefeng Bridge

Shuixi Village, Linjiang Town, Pucheng County, Fujian Province, built in 1809 AD.

This is a timber frame covered bridge, its log beams supported by four timber columns. It is covered by a multiple-eave overhanging gable roof. Two layers of skirts run along the bridge, protecting it from the rain. Its columns are painted with red lacquer, and their top and bottom portions are narrower than their middles.

家坛桥

福建省松溪县渭田镇董坑村,清嘉庆(1796—1820年)

单孔石拱木质廊桥,双坡顶覆小青瓦。家坛桥的石拱并未处于中央,如此不对称的方式在其他地方不多见。家坛桥与同一乡镇的马登桥、大旺桥型制类同,应为一个门派的师徒建造。

Jiatan Bridge

Dongkeng Village, Weitian Town, Songxi County, Fujian Province, built during 1796-1820 AD.

Jiatan Bridge is a single-span stone arch timber structure covered bridge. Its double-slope roof is covered with small grey tiles. The bridge's arch is not in the center of the bridge, an asymmetric style rarely seen in other places. Jiatan Bridge, together with Madeng Bridge, and Dawang Bridge are located in the same area, have a similar style, and should be built by the same group of craftsmen.

德胜桥

福建省建瓯市迪口镇郑魏村,清光绪二十五年(1899年)

又名胜桥。全木结构单拱廊桥,长36米、宽4.2米、高7.5米、跨径23米,十五开间。神龛供奉真武大帝神像。五脊悬山顶铺小青瓦。为市级文物保护单位。

Desheng Bridge

Zhengwei Village, Dikou Town, Jian'ou, Fujian Province, built in 1899 AD.

Also named Shengqiao Bridge, Desheng Bridge is a timber arch covered bridge. It has a gallery house with 15 bays. It is 36 meters long, 4.2 meters wide, and 7.5 meters high. It has a span of 23 meters. There is a shrine dedicated to the Zhenwu Emperor (a Taoist deity). It is covered by a five-ridge overhanging gable roof covered with small grey tiles. It has been listed as a historical and cultural sites protected at the municipal level.

种善桥

福建省南平市延平区茫荡镇盖头村高地自然村，清光绪二十九年（1903年）

清《闽小记》载："闽中桥梁最为巨丽，桥上建屋翼翼楚楚，无处不堪图画。"石块平梁、独跨全木结构楼阁式廊桥，长19米、宽4.4米、高8米、跨径7.2米。一说始建于唐代（618—907年），但未见史据。为县级文物保护单位。

Zhongshan Bridge

Gaodi Natural Village, Gaitou Village, Mangdang Town, Yanping District, Nanping, Fujian Province, built in 1903 AD.

It is stated in *A Brief Record of Fujian* written in the Qing Dynasty: "The Bridges of Fujian are magnificent and everywhere boast distinctive pavilions, with no place less wondrous than a painting." The approach to the bridge is made of stone and supported by crossbeams. It has a single span and a timber frame, built as a pavilion style covered bridge. It is 19 meters long, 4.4 meters wide, and 8 meters high. It has a span of 7.2 meters. It is said that the bridge was initially built in the Tang Dynasty (618-907 AD), but there is no proof of this. It has been listed as a historical and cultural sites protected at the county level.

后建桥

福建省建瓯市迪口镇可建村深溪自然村，清光绪三十二年（1906年）

全木结构伸臂式独拱廊桥，长30米、宽4米、高5米，十二开间。正梁遗存"大清光绪丙午叁十二年季冬月十三日巳时生梁"墨迹。1976年，各界人士捐资修缮。后建桥连接的古道已废弃，廊桥以及周围山谷有野猪、猕猴、山鸡出没。2006年，不法商贩盗走廊架十多根金丝楠木主梁，乡民使用竹竿、木柱支撑整座廊屋，后修缮。

Houjian Bridge

Shenxi Natural Village, Kejian Village, Dikou Town, Jian'ou, Fujian Province, built in 1906 AD.

Houjian Bridge is a timber cantilever bridge with a single arch. Its gallery house has 12 bays. It is 30 meters long, 4 meters wide, and 5 meters high. Characters written on its main beam state that "The beam was placed during the time period between nine and eleven o'clock in the morning on the thirteenth day of the eleventh lunar month in the 32nd year of the Emperor Guangxu period in the Qing Dynasty." The bridge was renovated in 1976 with funds collected by people from all walks of life. The ancient road that once connected to the Houjian Bridge has become overgrown, and wild boars, macaques, and pheasants now occupy the valley around the bridge. In 2006, a dozen or so bridge beams made of nanmu wood were stolen by criminal peddlers. Villagers then used bamboo poles and timber columns to support the entire gallery house. Repairs were subsequently made on the bridge.

高地桥

福建省南平市延平区茫荡镇盖头村高地自然村,清代(1644—1911年)

又名接龙桥。1942年重建,全木质结构,悬山顶覆小青瓦。茫荡山至黄石山距宝珠岭约有30米间隔。

Gaodi Bridge

Gaodi Natural Village, Gaitou Village, Mangdang Town, Yanping District, Nanping, Fujian Province, built during 1644-1911 AD.

Also named Jielong Bridge. Gaodi Bridge is a timber frame covered bridge, was rebuilt in 1942 AD. Its overhanging gable roof is covered by small grey tiles. The area that extends from the Mangdang to Huangshi Mountains is separated by a gap of about 30 meters from Baozhu Mountain ("Jewel Hill").

清代 1644—1911年

三溪桥

福建省闽侯县大湖乡六锦村与坂头村交界山谷，清道光二十四年（1844年）

雪溪、乌溪、凌云溪汇流桥下，故名三溪桥。又名蔡峰桥，自古是进出大山的唯一通道。距村六公里，连通闽县、侯官、罗源、闽清、古田五县交通。三溪桥建在火山岩形成的悬崖绝壁之间，长32米、宽5.4米、高3.7米，十二开间，距河床10余米。2016年，台风"莫兰蒂"裹挟狂风暴雨，特大洪水冲毁闽侯县四座木拱廊桥，其中有三溪桥。

Sanxi Bridge

in a valley between Liujin Village and Bantou Village, Dahu Township, Minhou County, Fujian Province, built in 1844 AD.

Sanxi Bridge gets its name from the three streams flowing under it—the Xuexi Stream, Wuxi Stream, and Lingyun Stream. Also named Caifeng Bridge, since ancient times it has served as the only path allowing people to come and go from the mountains. The bridge is located 6 kilometers away from the village, serving as an intersection of five counties including Minxian, Houguan, Luoyuan, Minqing and Gutian. It spans between cliff precipices formed out of volcanic rock. It is 32 meters long, 5.4 meters wide, 3.7 meters high, and sits over 10 meters above the river bed below. Its gallery house has 12 bays. In 2016, Typhoon Meranti struck Fujian. Especially large flood waters struck and destroyed four covered bridges in Minhou County. Among them was Sanxi Bridge.

岭下桥

福建省闽侯县大湖乡六锦村岭下自然村，清代（1644—1911年）

岭下桥是村庄交通要道。单跨八字木架支撑式廊桥，长9.6米、宽4.6米、跨径6.8米。支架上方另架贯木平梁，再上是桥面板。由8根砖柱、8根木柱支撑起廊顶，五脊悬山顶覆小青瓦，另覆压瓦锭。桥廊无墙，只设护栏，开敞式结构。

Lingxia Bridge

Lingxia Natural Village, Liujin Village, Dahu Township, Minhou County, Fujian Province, built during 1644-1911 AD.

Lingxia Bridge serves as an important node for traffic. The single-span covered bridge is supported by *bazi* bracing. On top of this support is another frame of interconnecting horizontal timber beams. On top of this are the floor boards of the bridge deck. The bridge is 9.6 meters long, 4.6 meters wide, and has a span of 6.8 meters. The gallery house is covered by a five-ridge overhanging gable roof topped with small grey tiles. The roof is supported by eight brick columns and by eight timber columns. The gallery house is an open structure without walls and has only a protective railing on either side.

安仁桥

福建省永安市青水畲族乡三房畲族村，清雍正二年（1724年）

原为独墩两孔平梁全木结构廊桥，后因河道变窄，桥墩逐渐靠附河岸，现为单孔，只有一半桥段跨小河。长55米、宽5米、高6米。两侧安置遮雨护板，有供行人歇息的长凳。两端桥头建歇山顶门庭，廊顶中部建三面双飞檐挑角阁楼。廊屋中央藻井为卯榫拱券式样。

清代 1644—1911年

Anren Bridge

Sanfang She Ethnic Village, Qingshui She Ethnic Township, Yongan, Fujian Province, built in 1724 AD.

This bridge was originally a multi-span, simply supported timber beam covered bridge with one pier and two spans. Later, due to the narrowing of the river, the bridge pier gradually approached the riverbank. It is now a single-span bridge with only half of the structure spanning the river. The bridge is 55 meters long, 5 meters wide, and 6 meters high. Awnings are installed on both sides, and benches are placed inside on which pedestrians can rest. Both ends of the bridge have a gatehouse with hip and gable roofs. In the middle of the bridge there is a three-sided pavilion with double-upturned-eaves and protruding corners. Mortise and tenon joins are used to build the arch-style caisson *zaojing* ceiling in the center of the gallery house.

化龙桥 / Hualong Bridge

福建省永安市青水畲族乡沧海畲族村，清乾隆元年（1736年）

Canghai She Ethnic Village, Qingshui She Ethnic Township, Yongan, Fujian Province, built in 1736 AD.

化龙桥为单孔木平梁结构廊桥，长28米、宽7米、高8米，八开间，是集桥梁、庙龛、戏台于一体的多功能建筑，是畲族古代乡土建筑的精华。为省级文物保护单位。

Hualong Bridge is a single-span wooden flat-beam covered bridge, measuring 28 meters in length, 7 meters in width, and 8 meters in height. Its gallery house has 8 bays. It serves as a multifunctional structure that integrates a bridge, shrine, and stage, representing the essence of ancient She ethnic architecture. It has been listed as a historical and cultural sites protected at the provincal level.

玉沙桥 / Yusha Bridge

福建省连城县四堡镇花溪河，清康熙二十三年（1684年）

Huaxi River, Sibao Town, Liancheng County, Fujian Province, built in 1684 AD.

河床沙石晶如白玉，故名。发祥于南宋（1127—1279年）时期的四堡镇有四件宝：古书坊、古雕版、古民居、古廊桥。石墩木梁瓦屋廊桥，长30米、宽5米、高10米，桥面铺鹅卵石，两旁建有木栅栏和木凳，桥侧、桥头安置木制雨篷。廊顶三座双层飞檐阁楼高低错落，精致美观。船首式桥墩上架七层交叉重叠圆木承托桥身，安稳牢固。

The sand on the riverbed here shines like white jade, from which the bridge's name is derived. Sibao Town's history dates to the Southern Song Dynasty (1127-1279 AD). It is famous for its "four treasures"—its ancient bookstores, ancient woodblocks, ancient residences, and ancient covered bridges. This stone-pier timber-beam tiled-roof covered bridge is 30 meters long, 5 meters wide, and 10 meters high. The bridge deck is covered with cobblestones. It has timber railings and benches on both sides. Awnings to protect the bridge from the rain are installed at both sides of the bridge and at the bridge heads. Three two-story pavilions of different sizes with upturned eaves are both exquisite and well-arranged. On top of the ship bow shaped bridge piers are seven layers of overlapping logs, which support and stabilize the bridge body.

蛟潭桥

福建省宁化县水茜镇安寨村,清早期

独孔石拱廊桥,长 10.5 米、宽 3.2 米、高 4 米、跨径 3.2 米,七开间。全木穿斗式结构,顶梁、立柱、木枋等构件全部以榫卯形式扣合,坚固且便于维修。木质雨披下设置护栏、长凳。桥下碧潭水深数十米,是闽江八大发源地之一。赶场乡亲回家途中会在廊桥歇脚。

Jiaotan Bridge

Anzhai Village, Shuiqian Town, Ninghua County, Fujian Province, built in early Qing Dynasty.

This is a stone arch covered bridge with a single span. It is 10.5 meters long, 3.2 meters wide, 4 meters high, and has a span of 3.2 meters. Its gallery house has 7 bays and is a *chuandou* style structure. Its columns, beams, and other timber components are joined by mortise and tenons, which makes the bridge solid, stable, and easy to maintain. There are guardrails and benches under the wooden awnings. The blue pool that flows under the bridge is dozens of meters deep and is one of the eight headwaters that flow into the Minjiang River. Villagers on their way home will often rest on the bridge.

铭新桥

福建省德化县大铭乡大铭村，清雍正八年（1730年）

原名大铭桥。乡绅林君宝出资募集桥材，乡民捐物捐劳建造。木架结构平梁独孔廊桥，长30.8米、宽4米，八开间。小廊阁居中歇山顶双重翘角飞檐，正中安置七级宝塔，两边各有奔腾彩龙。廊道两侧双重木制雨披下安置长凳。铭新桥多次被山洪冲毁又多次复建，最近一次大修是1938年。目前保护完好，仍然是大铭村通往外界的要道。铭新桥坐北朝南，东西各依山岗，满目翠绿陪衬一抹桥红。

Mingxin Bridge

Daming Village, Daming Township, Dehua County, Fujian Province, built in 1730 AD.

Originally known as Daming Bridge, this bridge was funded by Lin Junbao, a member of the local gentry, and the materials and labor were provided by local villagers. It is a simply supported timber beam covered bridge with a single span. It is 30.8 meters long, 4 meters wide, and has a gallery house with 8 bays. It has a hip and gable roof with double-upturned corners and upturned eaves. In the center there is a seven story pagoda, decorated on either side with sculptures of a dragon. Under the two-layer wooden awnings are benches. Mingxin Bridge was rebuilt several times after being destroyed by floods. It was most recently overhauled in 1938 AD. Now, this well-preserved bridge still serves as an important passageway between the village and the outside world. Looking out north from the bridge, can enjoy a view of hills from east to west, filling one's vision with verdant green together with a splash of red from the bridge.

溪边桥

福建省仙游县菜溪乡溪边村，清道光二十八年（1848年）

溪边桥位于村内象溪旁，又名桥内桥，1964年重修，南北走向，长31米、宽4.8米、高7.5米、跨径22米。现仍为村民进出村庄的重要通道。

Xibian Bridge

Xibian Village, Caixi Township, Xianyou County, Fujian Province, built in 1848 AD.

Xibian Bridge, located within the village and adjacent to the creek, is also known as Qiaonei Bridge. It was rebuilt in 1964 and runs in a south-north direction. It is 31 meters long, 4.8 meters wide, and 7.5 meters high, with a span of 22 meters. It remains an important passage for villagers to enter and exit the village.

宴林口桥

福建省德化县盖德镇林地村,清代(1644—1911年)

唐代至新中国成立前,德化县二百余座瓷窑分布在偏僻山村,以北宋盖德镇"碗砰仑窑"为代表烧制各种白瓷。林地村又称宴林口,是山地窑场制品东运泉州港外销的重要通道。宋代建简易木桥,清乾隆四十七年(1782年)改建为廊桥。一墩两孔木平廊桥,长27.3米、宽3.4米、高3.95米。两侧设长板坐凳,外侧敷设双层雨披板,直脊对称三叠悬山顶覆青杂瓦。清光绪三十年(1904年)水毁,乡绅林仁礼捐家财重建。1959年修缮加固。

Yanlinkou Bridge

Lindi Village, Gaide Town, Dehua County, Fujian Province, built during 1644-1911 AD.

From 618 AD to 1949 AD, over 200 kilns for producing porcelain operated in remote mountain villages throughout Dehua County. During the Northern Song Dynasty, the "Wanpenglun Kiln" in Gaide Town was renowned for its production of all sorts of white porcelain. Lindi Village (also known as Yanlin Kou) served as an important node for the goods of the mountain kilns along their way to export from the port of Quanzhou. At this village, a simply supported timber bridge was constructed during the Song Dynasty. It was rebuilt as a covered bridge in 1782 AD. It has one pier and two spans and is a timber frame covered bridge. It is 27.3 meters long, 3.4 meters wide, and 3.95 meters high. On both sides of the bridge are benches, and outside the bridge is a double-level awning. The bridge is covered by a three-layered symmetrical overhanging gable roof and is topped with assorted grey tiles. The bridge was destroyed by a flood in 1904 AD, after which Lin Renli, a member of the local gentry, donated his family's wealth to rebuild it. In 1959, the bridge was completely repaired and reinforced.

龙门桥

安徽省太湖县北中镇马嘶村望天河，清道光二十五年（1845年）

平梁木结构廊桥，长14米、宽4.6米、高3.5米，五开间，东西走向。内侧置美人靠坐凳和木制栏杆，桥身外侧安置防雨翼板，桥面由方木条卯榫铺砌。两端各建一小间青砖小瓦龙脊桥头堡，石头垒筑，石缝用桐油石灰浆砌。是皖西南仅存的古代廊桥，受到百姓珍爱。为县级文物保护单位。

Longmen Bridge

Wangtian River, Masi Village, Beizhong Town, Taihu County, Anhui Province, built in 1845 AD.

This single-span, simply supported timber beam bridge is 14 meters long, 4.6 meters wide, and 3.5 meters high. Its gallery house has 5 bays. Benches with chair backs and timber railings are set inside the bridge, and rain-proof boards are installed outside the bridge. The deck is covered with timber boards fastened together with mortise and tenons. At both ends of the bridge, there are small bridgeheads built with grey bricks and small tiles, with mortar formed of tung oil and calcium hydroxide. Longmen Bridge is the only ancient covered bridge that remains in Southwest Anhui Province, and it is cherished by the people here. It has been listed as a historical and cultural sites protected at the county level.

麟清桥

江西省婺源县浙源乡十堡村，清道光二十三年（1843年）

桥下河水清澈，一群鱼儿悠然自得，鳞片的幽光清晰可见，故桥名为"鳞清"，亦称"麟清"。原为木平梁全木结构廊桥，后因村民维修时珍惜树木，将木梁改为水泥梁，保留敞廊式穿斗结构、木柱瓦顶的古貌。桥长22米、宽3米、高4.2米。

Linqing Bridge

Shibao Village, Zheyuan Township, Wuyuan County, Jiangxi Province, built in 1843 AD.

The water below Linqing Bridge is clear, and fish leisurely swim there, the light green shade of their scales clearly visible. As a result, the bridge was named Linqing Bridge. Originally, this was a simply supported timber beam covered bridge. Later, because villagers highly valued timber during repairs, they replaced the timber beams with cement ones and retained the bridge's open gallery house *chuandou* style structure, as well as its ancient appearance, through the use of tiles and timber columns. The bridge is 22 meters long, 3 meters wide, and 4.2 meters high.

永镇桥

江西省安远县新龙乡江头村甲江河,清顺治九年（1652年）

　　又名五渡水瓦桥,清顺治九年（1652年）僧人欧阳融募化桥资建造,后遭水毁,清乾隆十四年（1749年）乡民广捐木石予以重建。长38.5米、宽4.33米、高8米,两墩三孔木平廊桥。船首形桥墩,顶似鸟喙,客家人称其为"鹅胸"。为省级文物保护单位。

Yongzhen Bridge

Jiajiang River, Jiangtou Village, Xinlong Township, Anyuan County, Jiangxi Province, built in 1652 AD.

Yongzhen Bridge, also named Wudu Shuiwa Bridge, was built with alms collected by a monk named Ouyang Rong in 1652 AD. The bridge was destroyed by a flood and was rebuilt in 1749 AD with wood and stone donated by local villagers. The bridge has two piers and three spans. It is a timber beam covered bridge that is 38.5 meters long, 4.33 meters wide, and 8 meters high. Its piers have the shape of a ship bow with the point resembling a beak, which Hakka people call a goose breast. It has been listed as a historical and cultural relic sites protected at the provincial level.

韩家庄桥

江西省婺源县紫阳镇齐村韩家庄村，清代（1644—1911年）

一条无名小河丝带一般缠绕着韩家庄村，偶尔有打鱼的小船悄悄划过水面。河岸两侧森林茂密，从远处看似朵朵绿色的云。韩家庄桥是一座两孔廊桥，坐落在村子小河出口上。

Hanjiazhuang Bridge

Hanjiazhuang Village, Qicun Village, Ziyang Town, Wuyuan County, Jiangxi Province, built during 1644-1911 AD.

An unnamed river winds around much of Hanjiazhuang Village like a silk ribbon. One can occasionally see fishing boats quietly paddling across the waters here. On either riverbank, one can see dense forests that look like green clouds from a distance. At the point where the river exits the village, there is a covered bridge with two spans.

永宁桥

江西省石城县高田镇上柏村,清乾隆三年(1738年)

单孔石拱楼阁式廊桥,长34米、宽5.2米、高4.4米、跨径10.6米、十二开间。永宁桥坚实牢固,古朴大方。中部亭阁设神龛,供奉关公神像。桥基由麻石砌筑,穿斗式全木结构,外侧设置木板可遮风雨,歇山顶覆小青瓦。为省级文物保护单位。

Yongning Bridge

Shangbai Village, Gaotian Town, Shicheng County, Jiangxi Province, built in 1738 AD.

This single-span stone arch pavilion covered bridge is 34 meters long, 5.2 meters wide, and 4.4 meters high. It has a span of 10.6 meters. Its gallery house is a timber *chuandou* style structure with 12 bays. The structure is solid, firm, simple, and elegant. The pavilion in the middle of the bridge has a shrine dedicated to Guan Yu, a general from the Three Kingdoms period, worshipped as a deity. The bridge has a hip and gable roof covered with small grey tiles, and the bridge's foundation is constructed of granite. It has been listed as a historical and cultural sites protected at the provincial level.

玉带桥

江西省信丰县虎山乡中心村虎山河，清乾隆五年（1740年）

玉带桥以"一弯澄水镜，半壁佩玉带"的弧状桥形得名。连通赣南客家聚集区通往粤北、闽西、湘南商贸古驿道。两墩三孔石拱楼阁式廊桥。桥墩青石砌筑，状如船首，跨径14.3米。桥体弧长88.15米、弦长74.44米，弧弦最大距离10.84米，宽3.8米，三十二开间。两端各建4.2米高砖瓦桥头堡。为省级文物保护单位。

Yudai Bridge

Hushan River, Zhongxin Village, Hushan Township, Xinfeng County, Jiangxi Province, built in 1740 AD.

Yudai Bridge gets its name from its curved bridge shape, which is like "a round mirror reflecting clear water, the form of half of a jade belt". The bridge was part of the ancient trade and courier route that connected Hakka settlements in southern Jiangxi Province with north Guangdong, west Fujian, and south Hunan. The stone arch pavilion style covered bridge has two piers and three spans. It is supported by bluestone piers that have the shape of ship bows. The bridge has an arch length of 88.15 meters, and a chord length of 74.44 meters, with a maximum distance between the arch and chord of 10.84 meters. It is 3.8 meters wide and has clear spans of 14.3 meters. Its gallery house has 32 bays. Each end of the bridge has a 4.2 meters brick-tile bridge tower. The bridge has been listed as a historical and cultural sites protected at the provincial level.

初石桥

江西省定南县鹅公镇柱石村,清同治十二年(1873年)

双坡顶八角灯塔式廊桥,连通赣南至粤东古驿道。又名柱石桥。桥长16米、宽5米、高16米。桥基、桥面使用桐油拌和石灰浆黏合条石,坚固如磐,二层阁楼设置神龛供奉真武大帝。《重修初石桥序》碑记:"清光绪乙酉年(1885年)、民国十五年(1926年)、1987年重修。初石桥是本地最早建造的单拱石桥,故称初石桥。是我县仅存的桥亭结构建筑物。"

Chushi Bridge

Zhushi Village, Egong Town, Dingnan County, Jiangxi Province, built in 1873 AD.

Chushi Bridge is a double-slope eight-corner lighthouse-style covered bridge. It connected the ancient courier route that linked southern Jiangxi to eastern Guangdong. Also known as Zhushi Bridge, the bridge is 16 meters long, 5 meters wide, and 16 meters high. Its foundation and deck are held together with a mixture of tung oil and lime, which makes the structure solid and strong. A shrine in the pavilion on the second floor is dedicated to Zhenwu (a Taoist deity). As stated in the *Preface for the Reconstruction of the First Stone Bridge*, "the bridge was the first single-span stone arch bridge built in this area. It was thus called Chushi Bridge. It was rebuilt in 1885 AD, 1926 AD, and 1987. It is also the only pavilion bridge left in our county."

永安桥

江西省赣州市南康区莲花河，清光绪（1875—1908 年）

据《钟氏族谱》记载，以"永以为好既安且吉"确定桥名。永安桥由石墩、石梁、石柱、砖门、木枋、瓦顶组成，为一墩两孔叠梁式平梁廊桥。叠梁承载上部结构，长 13.2 米、宽 4 米。桥廊两侧安置长条木凳护栏，四根方石柱挺拔坚固。廊柱遗留两副古联"永留司马题斯柱，安得重阳卧此桥""永怀冀免褰裳者，安坐何须纳履人"，将"永安"两字藏嵌其中。

Yongan Bridge

Lianhua River, Nankang District, Ganzhou, Jiangxi Province, built during 1875-1908 AD.

As recorded in *The Genealogy of the Zhong Lineage*, the name Yongan (eternal peace in Chinese) Bridge is derived from the statement "for eternal peace and auspiciousness". The bridge is composed of stone piers, stone beams, stone columns, a brick gate, timber architraves, and tiles. It has one pier and two spans and is a combined beam style simply supported beam covered bridge. The combined beams support the upper structure. It is 13.2 meters long and 4 meters wide. It is equipped with long benches and guardrails on both sides. Its four rectangular stone columns are strong and steady. There is a couplet on the columns, which includes the characters "eternal" and "peace" are concealed within the verse.

清代 1644—1911 年

太平桥

江西省龙南市杨村镇车田村太平江,清代(1644—1911年)

现桥于清嘉庆元年(1796年)重建。桥长44.8米、宽4米、高约15.2米,两孔跨径为11.9米、12.9米,拱高6.2米。花岗石一墩两块,桐油、石灰、红糖、糯米浆为灰浆砌筑。砖石结构,大跨径拱形四通桥亭,长30米、高10米。亭顶有三对翘角飞檐,顶覆小青瓦。为全国重点文物保护单位。

Taiping Bridge

Taiping River in Chetian Village, Yangcun Town, Longnan, Jiangxi Province, built during 1644-1911 AD.

The existing bridge was rebuilt in 1796 AD. The bridge is 44.8 meters long, 4 meters wide, and about 15.2 meters high. Its two spans are 11.9 meters and 12.9 meters long. The height of its arch is 6.2 meters. The bridge is built with granite, has one pier and two approaches, and uses tung oil, lime, brown sugar and glutinous rice to serve as mortar. On the bridge deck, there is a pavilion built with bricks and stones and composed of a large-span arch. The pavilion is 30 meters long, 10 meters high. The pavilion roof has three pairs of protruding corners with upturned eaves and is covered by small grey tiles. The bridge has been listed as a historical and cultural sites protected at the national level.

三川桥

江西省崇仁县许坊乡三川桥村，清乾隆（1736—1795年）

石拱独孔木结构廊桥，长12米、宽3.8米、高4米、跨径4米，七开间。桥面坡度较大，台阶由独轮车道隔为左右，上下往来两侧不相干扰。桥廊支柱、横梁、檐枋等构件的衔接采用榫卯结构，清末大修一次。三川桥是崇仁县仅存的古代廊桥，整体构造为国内廊桥罕见，对于研究古代桥梁技术、建筑工艺、区域文化具有重要价值。

Sanchuan Bridge

Sanchuanqiao Village, Xufang Township, Chongren County, Jiangxi Province, built during 1736-1795 AD.

This single-span stone arch covered bridge is 12 meters long, 3.8 meters wide, and 4 meters high. It has a gallery house with 7 bays and a span of 4 meters. The bridge deck has a steep slope, and its steps have two grooves for wheelbarrows on the right and on the left so that people going up the bridge won't be disturbed by those going down. The gallery house uses supportive columns, transverse beams, architraves, and other components, which are all joined by mortise and tenon technology. The bridge was once overhauled at the end of the Qing Dynasty. Sanchuan Bridge is the only ancient covered bridge that survives in Chongren County, and it demonstrates unique construction that is rarely seen elsewhere in China. As a result, it is of significant value in the research of ancient bridge construction techniques, craftsmanship, and reginal culture.

万寿桥

江西省广昌县塘坊镇村里村,清道光元年(1821年)

《广昌县志》记:"万寿桥始建于一八二一年(清道光元年),广昌十景之一。初为纯木构造鸦雀薮桥,后因屡遭水患,历时三年,耗银九千余元改为石墩拱桥。"三孔联拱砖石廊桥,长66米、宽5米、高7米,三孔跨径均为13米。桥墩使用长方体石块砌筑,迎水面为舰首形,顶尖鹰喙用于分解洪水。砖石廊道两端门厅装饰马头墙飞檐,中部顶端建四角挑檐小阁。

Wanshou Bridge

Cunli Village, Tangfang Town, Guangchang County, Jiangxi Province, built in 1821 AD.

It is recorded in *The History of Guangchang County* that "Wanshou Bridge, one of the ten scenic spots in Guangchang, was built in 1821 AD. It was at first a pure timber bridge but was reconstructed into a stone arch bridge after repeated floods. The construction took three years at a cost of more than 9,000 silver dollars." The bridge is 66 meters long, 5 meters wide, and 7 meters high. Each of its three spans is 13 meters long. The piers are made of rectangular stones, and their upstream-facing sides are shaped in the form of a ship bow, with "eagle beak" points used to lessen the impact of flood waters. Both ends of the brick gallery house are decorated with horse-head walls with upturned eaves. In the center, there is a small pavilion with a four-corner roof sporting upturned eaves.

玉带桥

浙江省杭州市西湖，清雍正九年（1731年）

桥碑记载，浙江总督李卫建玉带桥，为亭式廊桥，石墩石台木柱歇山顶，两墩三孔上斜石阶，重檐翘角廊亭覆小青瓦，汉白玉栏杆雕刻龙凤波涛、莲叶荷花。1912—1949年间损毁，1983年文物部门按照原桥尺度式样修复。"玉带晴虹"是清代西湖十八景之一。

Yudai Bridge

West Lake, Hangzhou, Zhejiang Province, built in 1731 AD.

According to the bridge's stele, the Yudai Bridge was built by Li Wei, the governor of Zhejiang. It is a pavilion type covered bridge with stone piers and abutments, along with timber columns and a hip and gable roof. It has two piers and three spans, as well as slanted stone steps. Its multiple-eave pavilion roof has upturned corners and is covered with small grey tiles. Its "han white jade" (*hanbaiyu*) protective wall is carved with dragons, phoenixes, waves, lotus flowers, and lotus leaves. It was damaged during 1912-1949 AD. In 1983, the department of cultural relics restored the bridge according to its original scale and design. The "Jade Belt and Sunny Rainbow" is one of the eighteen scenic spots of the West Lake dating to the Qing Dynasty.

卧波桥

浙江省宁波市奉化区萧王庙街道袁家岙村龙溪,清乾隆二十四年(1759年)

袁家岙村《袁氏宗谱》记,清乾隆二十四年(1759年)族人"叠木为梁,架分七进",建造了一座楼阁式木梁廊桥,长24米、宽6.4米。

Wobo Bridge

Longxi Creek, Yuanjia'ao Village, Xiaowangmiao Sub-district, Fenghua District, Ningbo, Zhejiang Province, built in 1759 AD.

The Genealogy of the Yuan Family records that in 1759 AD, lineage members built a pavilion-style timber beam covered bridge, with combined timbers serving as beams. It is 24 meters long and 6.4 meters wide.

逢源双桥

浙江省桐乡市乌镇镇，清代（1644—1911年）

两墩三孔、石梁石阶、木柱木梁穿斗式廊桥，长16米、宽4米、高6米，六开间。桥下铁栅是水流关卡，左右两桥合并故称双桥。桥廊中央筑1.5米高青砖隔墙，上部由通顶木质花窗分隔，两桥下部各有两道石栏。传说男女并行难免滋生尴尬，故有男左女右过桥的习俗。另有来走左边、往走右边，左右逢源升官发财之说。

Fengyuan Shuangqiao Bridge

Wuzhen Town, Tongxiang, Zhejiang Province, built during 1644-1911 AD.

This is a two pier and three span bridge with stone beams and stone steps, as well as *chuandou* style gallery house with timber columns and timber beams. It is 16 meters long, 4 meters wide, and 6 meters high. Its gallery house has 6 bays. Under the bridge there is an iron grid used to stem the flow of water. Since the bridge is formed by two adjacent bridges, it is called a double bridge. In the center of the gallery house, a 1.5-meter-high grey brick partition wall is constructed, with its upper part separated by a wooden window. There are two stone fences at the lower part of the two bridges. It is said that on this bridge, men would pass left while women would pass right to avoid causing embarrassment by walking together.

三亭桥

江苏省苏州市吴江区同里镇,清代(1644—1911 年)

同里位于古运河东,由 5 个淡水湖分离为 7 个小岛,49 座古桥连为一体,三亭桥是唯一的廊桥,为"小桥、流水、人家"典型景致。因水隔桥连成就了共同的乡里,故名同里。桥块由河岸伸展进入河中数米,上架条石为梁,两侧有护栏。4 根直立、斜立木柱支撑 3 个青瓦廊亭。两边廊亭略小,为歇山顶。中亭较大,攒尖顶竖立宝珠钮。桥坡石阶高 5.8 米、宽 2.6 米、长 13 米。

Santing Bridge

Tongli Town, Wujiang District, Suzhou, Jiangsu Province, built during 1644-1911 AD.

Tongli is located to the east of an ancient canal. It is separated by five freshwater lakes into seven islands. Forty-nine ancient bridges are connected together here. Santing Bridge is the only covered bridge among them. The bridge projects several meters into the water from its base on the shore, and stones are rested on top to serve as beams. Protective guardrails are placed on both sides of the bridge. Four upright and four oblique timber columns are used to support three tiled pavilions. The pavilions on either side of the bridge are slightly smaller than that at the center, and are covered by hip and gable roofs. The central pavilion is relatively big and has a cone-shaped roof. The stone steps on the bridge slope are 5.8 meters high, 2.6 meters wide, and 13 meters long.

五亭桥

江苏省扬州市瘦西湖莲花堤，清乾隆二十二年（1757年）

　　为恭迎圣驾，巡盐御史高恒主持盐商襄赞，于乾隆皇帝第二次南巡前夕建成此桥。又名莲花桥，长55米，跨径7.13米的中心桥洞与12座桥洞相通。桥阶下另设两孔扇形桥洞。桥面中亭为重檐四角攒尖式宝亭，亭顶坡度较陡，向上呈尖锥状，四条垂脊交会于宝顶。翼亭为单檐攒尖式，置中亭周围。

Wuting Bridge

Lianhua Dam of the Slender West Lake, Yangzhou, Jiangsu Province, built in 1757 AD.

In order to greet the "sacred throne", Gao Heng, a inspector of salt revenue, presided over the construction of Wuting Bridge on the eve of Emperor Qianlong's second Southern Tour. Another name of the bridge is Lianhua Bridge, and it is 55 meters long. Its central archway is 7.13 meters long and is connected with another 12 archways. There are another two fan-shaped archways set underneath the bridge steps. The pavilion in the center of the bridge deck is slightly higher than the other pavilions that have multiple-eave, four-corner roofs and protruding tops.

后 记

为进一步展示中国交通运输发展不平凡的历程，传承和发扬中华优秀传统文化，人民交通出版社策划出版《中国廊桥精粹》一书。

本书编写力求科学严谨、求真务实。郑皆连院士作为本书编写组主任，交通运输部公路科学研究院原院长张劲泉、上海交通大学教授刘杰作为副主任，对书稿进行了审核；湖南省交通运输厅编志办主任蒋响元、中国国家博物馆终身研究馆员杨林、江西赣粤高速公路股份有限公司副总经理漆志平、福建省海员工会副主席金宁帆等提出了宝贵意见。原《中国交通报》记者吴卫平通过20余年实地踏勘，考察记录廊桥540余座，为本书编写倾注了大量心血。

人民交通出版社对本书的出版非常重视，给予大力支持，社领导舒驰、刘韬就书稿的内容框架多次提出宝贵意见，韩亚楠、齐黄柏盈、陈鹏、郭晓旭、单籽跃等同志为本书编辑做了大量工作。

受编写资料和篇幅所限，本书难免挂一漏万，存在不足之处，欢迎广大读者提出宝贵意见、建议，便于我们及时修订完善，以期更好地宣传好、展示好中国廊桥这块璀璨夺目的交通文化瑰宝！

编者

2024年9月

EPILOGUE

To further demonstrate the remarkable journey of China's transportation development and inherit and promote China's fine traditional culture, China Communications Press planned to publish the book *The Quintessence of Covered Bridges in China*.

The writing of this book strives for scientific rigor and a pragmatic pursuit of truth. Academician Zheng Jielian, as the chair of the Compilation Committee, and Zhang Jingquan, former director of the Research Institute of Highway of the Ministry of Transport, and Liu Jie, professor of Shanghai Jiaotong University, as the vice-chairs of the Compilation Committee, carefully reviewed and revised the manuscript. Jiang Xiangyuan, director of the History and Records Office of the Department of Transportation of Hunan Province, Yang Lin, a lifelong researcher at the National Museum of China, Qi Zhiping, deputy general manager of Jiangxi Gan-Yue Expressway Co., Ltd., Jin Ningfan, deputy chairman of the Seamen's Union of Fujian Province, and others offered valuable suggestions.

Wu Weiping, a former reporter of China Transport News, has devoted a lot of efforts to the compilation of this book through more than 20 years of field surveys and inspection records of more than 540 covered bridges.

China Communications Press attaches great importance to the publication of this book, and its management Shu Chi and Liu Tao have offered valuable opinions and suggestions on multiple occasions. Han Yanan, Qi-Huang Baiying, Chen Peng, Guo Xiaoxu, Shan Ziyue and other colleagues did a lot of work for the editing of this book.

Due to the limitation of compilation materials and space, there are inevitably deficiencies in this book. We welcome readers to put forward valuable opinions and suggestions so that we can better display the dazzling treasure of China's covered bridges.

Editors
September 2024

图书在版编目（CIP）数据

中国廊桥精粹：汉文、英文 /《中国廊桥精粹》编写组主编. — 北京：人民交通出版社股份有限公司, 2024.9. — ISBN 978-7-114-19697-3

Ⅰ. K928.78

中国国家版本馆 CIP 数据核字第 2024WS8529 号

本书由人民交通出版社独家出版发行。未经著作权人书面许可，本书图片及文字任何部分，不得以任何方式和手段进行复制、转载或刊登。版权所有，侵权必究。

Copyright © 2024

All rights reserved. No part of this publication may be reproduced, stored in a retrieval system, or transmitted in any form or by any means, electronic, mechanical, photocopying, recording or otherwise, without the prior written permission of the copyright holder. Printed in China.

Zhongguo Langqiao Jingcui

书　　名：	中国廊桥精粹
著 作 者：	《中国廊桥精粹》编写组
责任编辑：	韩亚楠　齐黄柏盈　陈　鹏　郭晓旭　单籽跃
责任校对：	赵媛媛　龙　雪
责任印制：	刘高彤
出版发行：	人民交通出版社
地　　址：	（100011）北京市朝阳区安定门外外馆斜街3号
网　　址：	http://www.ccpcl.com.cn
销售电话：	(010)85285857
总 经 销：	人民交通出版社发行部
经　　销：	各地新华书店
印　　刷：	北京雅昌艺术印刷有限公司
开　　本：	965×635　1/8
印　　张：	30.5
字　　数：	310千
版　　次：	2024年9月　第1版
印　　次：	2024年9月　第1次印刷
书　　号：	ISBN 978-7-114-19697-3
定　　价：	398.00元

（有印刷、装订质量问题的图书，由本社负责调换）